# GOLDEN GIRLS

## True Stories of Olympic Women Stars

# CARLI LAKLAN

## McGRAW-HILL BOOK COMPANY

NEW YORK   ST. LOUIS   SAN FRANCISCO   AUCKLAND
BOGOTÁ   DÜSSELDORF   JOHANNESBURG   LONDON   MADRID
MEXICO   MONTREAL   NEW DELHI   PANAMA   PARIS
SÃO PAULO   SINGAPORE   SYDNEY   TOKYO   TORONTO

OCLC # 5706521
Library of Congress Cataloging in Publication Data

Laklan, Carli.
    Golden girls.

    SUMMARY: Brief biographies of women athletes who became
Olympic winners.
        1.  Athletes, Women—Biography—Juvenile literature.
    2.  Olympic games—History—Juvenile literature.
    [1.  Athletes. 2.  Olympic games—History] I.  Title.
GV697.A1L25        796'.092'2 [B]    [920]    79-24052
ISBN 0-07-036074-X

Book design by Earl Tidwell

1234567890MUMU87654321o

# GOLDEN
# GIRLS

*For Maggie,*
*a very special Golden Girl*

# ACKNOWLEDGMENTS

My sincere thanks to the Romanian Library, New York City; to the Embassy of the Union of Soviet Socialist Republics; to the Women's Sports Foundation, San Francisco; . . . to my research assistant, Bette Benfield; to the wonderful librarians of the New York City and Nassau County systems; to my husband, James Aiello, for his unstinting support and help; and to all those who aided me in getting the material for this book together.

# GOLDEN
# GIRLS

The huge Evanston, Illinois, stadium was packed with cheering spectators. Overhead the sun shone bright in a near-cloudless sky. Bands played and banners waved in a light breeze. It was July 16, 1932, and a perfect day for the Women's National Championship. Teams from all over the country had come to compete. Excitement ran high.

*"The Illinois Women's Athletic Team!"* The announcement blared from the loudspeakers. Applause swelled. One by one, twenty-two girl athletes advanced to center field as their names were called. The crowd went wild. These were the favorites!

Together they made their exit, and they looked invincible. Another fanfare sounded. *"The team from Dallas, Texas!"* People leaned forward, eager to see these new competitors who would challenge their favorites. And then they stared.

A single teen-aged girl marched alone to midfield, head high, short-cropped dark hair ruffled in the breeze, face lifted to receive her welcome from the audience.

"Mildred (Babe) Didrikson!" the announcer called.

There was a moment of dead silence. Then high up in the stands laughter began. It was picked up by others until the whole stadium rocked with it. One girl! One thin, gangly girl was the whole "team" from Texas! The laughter swelled higher.

It was like a slap in the face, that laughter. The girl's shoulders hunched for just one moment in bewildered reaction. She had never anticipated a greeting like this. She knew why she was alone: the Dallas club she belonged to couldn't afford to send more than one representative, and Babe was proud that she had been chosen. She had come determined to do her best for her club. And the crowd thought it a joke!

Babe's shoulders squared. Her chin came up a little higher. Turning with almost military precision, she marched from the field, the laughter trailing after her. Not for a second did she let her hurt show.

If she had been determined before, she was doubly so now. They could laugh at *her* if they wanted to, but they were making fun of her club, her city, the state that had sent her. And this she would not have! She would make them take that laughter back! She would show them that the team from Texas was no joke at all.

That afternoon Babe Didrikson did the impossible. There were ten events scheduled. She entered eight of them. She had no rest between them; often not enough time for a practice trial. She dashed from one event to another. She won the 80-meter hurdles, and then the broad jump. She took first place in the baseball throw, tied for first in the javelin, won the shotput though it was the first time she'd ever put a shot.

The crowd that had laughed grew quieter and quieter as she racked up the points. Another first in the high jump. She missed out on the 100-meter dash—she couldn't get there in time; she was too busy throwing the discus. She only got a fourth in that, but then, like the shotput, she had never tried it before. In other events she had already set three new world's records.

Grudgingly at first, and then with mounting acknowledgment of her prowess, the laughter turned to cheers. When the scores were tallied, Babe Didrikson had made 30 points—the Texas "team" had won first place in the meet. Coming in second were the twenty-two Illinois athletes, with 22 points. The spectators rose and gave Babe the standing ovation she well deserved.

Mildred Ella Didrikson, as she was christened,

was born in the small town of Port Arthur, Texas, the sixth of seven lively children. As a toddler she was called "Baby," but this soon changed to Babe, and that was the name the whole world would come to know her by.

Her Norwegian-born father had been a ship's carpenter and had sailed around Cape Horn at the very southern tip of South America nineteen times. What tales he could tell of those dangerous voyages, of ice floes and wild storms, about the penguins the crews sometimes sighted! Babe loved those stories, but there weren't too many evenings when her father could sit and tell them. When he retired from the sea and settled his growing family in Port Arthur, then later in Beaumont, he had become a cabinetmaker as well as a carpenter. It took long hours of not-always-easy-to-find work to make ends meet.

Babe's mother had been a champion skater in Norway, and both parents believed in physical training. All of their children were active, outdoors youngsters.

Babe was the best of them all. She had a natural talent for whatever sport she tried, and she tried most of them: swimming, riding, skating, diving, to name a few. By the time she was in grade school, she could outrun all of the girls and most of the boys, could outshoot them in basketball, outhit them in baseball.

"I had an urge to be first in everything," she said. Maybe not all of that urge came from competitiveness. As Babe grew toward her teen-age years, she felt secretly that she wasn't pretty and that boys didn't really like her, although they were willing to have her on their teams. Often she pretended she didn't care.

"I hate sissies!" she announced, and rushed to the backyard to practice weight lifting, using her mother's old-fashioned flatirons tied to a broomstick as makeshift weights. It was better than crying.

"I can whup you!" she shouted when she felt left out.

But sometimes she'd creep away and play the harmonica she had taught herself to make music on. Sometimes, late in the night, the sounds would drift from her small room into the Texas darkness, as though they were reaching out in loneliness, reaching for the friendships she felt "being plain" shut her away from.

Like everything else Babe did, she learned to play the harmonica expertly—so well that when she was seven a local radio station hired her to appear on a regular program. She held that job until she was ten.

By then she had made up her mind that she was going to make a career of sports. She was already a crack basketball player, though school rules barred her from team play until she entered high school. There her talent exploded. Babe spearheaded the team to championship.

She was a senior, playing in an interdistrict tournament, when she attracted the attention of Melvin J.

McCombs, coach of the Golden Cyclones, one of the best girls' teams in the country.

"How would you like to play with the Cyclones?" he asked her.

How would she like it? How does a cat like cream or a rabbit like carrots?

"But you'll have to leave school," her mother protested. "And graduation is so near."

"I'll keep up," Babe promised. "I'll do my lessons."

"There will be too much traveling," her father said flatly. "Better you stay in school. Learn to be a good typist. Then you get a good job."

"I can already type one hundred words a minute!" Babe cried. "Dad, listen—you don't understand! The Cyclones are sponsored by the Employers Casualty Company in Dallas. And the company will hire me as a clerk. I'll make seventy-five whole dollars a month!" That was good money in those days, and it would help out at home. Her father hesitated.

"You are only sixteen," her mother worried. "Too young for a girl——"

"I can take care of myself as well as any boy!" She doubled up her fists and planted her feet wide apart, looking as fierce as she possibly could. "I'm no sissy!"

"You would do better to try to make yourself prettier," her mother said tartly.

That stung, but Babe didn't show it. "I can sew," she argued. "And cook and do housework. Those are girl things!" She swung back to her father, sensing how much the money weighted his decision. "It's my chance!" she pleaded. "I'll work hard on the job, and they'll give me an even better one later. I'll just have a head start! Please, Papa! Please!"

And so it was arranged. Babe was given special permission to work—*if* she kept up her grades. It was a heavy schedule, with practice sessions, games, school-work, and a job. But Babe made it. In June she earned her diploma. She was the star of the Cyclones, and they took the U. S. National Tournament three years in a row. Twice Babe was named All-American forward. And on the side, she designed and made a sports dress that won first prize at the Texas State Fair. It was a very pretty dress!

Much as she loved basketball, Babe had another bee in her bonnet. She had first read about the Olympics when she was fourteen, and ever since she had dreamed of entering—and winning. She had practiced by herself: running, jumping makeshift hurdles, throwing a broomstick for a javelin—but she knew if her dream were to come true, she'd have to have far better training.

Coach McCombs seemed to be the answer. Babe marshaled her arguments and talked to company officials. She was persuasive. The track team was formed with McCombs as coach. Babe was the star.

She held the A.A.U. record in every track and field event she entered. She captained her track team to second place in the nation—and it was Babe who won the most points. She set eight track and field records for the South, and three for the nation. She broke four world records. She was a 126-pound, five-feet-six-and-a-half-inches-tall dynamo—who "hated sissies."

Inside there was a wistful, lonely girl. A very shy girl. There was to be a big party one night after a meet. Everyone was invited. Babe had made herself a special evening dress, using all her skill so it would be just right. She bought new shoes, too, with high heels. When she hung her dress in the locker room where the girls were to change after the meet, she let herself hope just a little that tonight she'd "belong."

After her shower Babe was by herself in a corner trying to fix her hair, feeling nervousness about the coming party creeping through her, pretending it wasn't there. The other girls were laughing and chattering, hurrying into their gowns, fixing their makeup, oblivious to Babe.

One of the girls flipped out the skirt of Babe's dress. "Keen," she said admiringly.

Another girl giggled. "But can you imagine *her* in it? She'll look like a scarecrow!"

"Come on! Come on! We don't want to be late!"

They fluttered out, never noticing Babe. The locker room was empty. Babe's dress hung alone. Slowly she moved to it and touched the soft fabric. She smoothed it gently. Two big tears she couldn't stop rolled down her cheeks.

She choked back sobs that wanted to come, folded the new dress slowly and put it back in its box. Outside she heard the sounds of music and happy laughter. In all of her life she had never felt so lonely.

More than ever now Babe kept to herself. She won the Women's National Championship that memorable day in Evanston. The Olympic Games lay less than a month ahead, and she was determined to win every event she could enter. It might not make up for the hurt, but it would help.

Then the Olympic officials made a new rule: no woman could enter more than three events! Babe was furious. "They saw me coming!" she snapped. Maybe they had. No competing nation would want their contestant to come up against Babe more times than were necessary.

There was a lot of worry about the Games being staged that year. The world was in the midst of a depression. How would Los Angeles, the host city, manage the cost? But manage it did, and magnificently. The main stadium had seats for 105,000 people, and those seats were filled every day. The swimming stadium was perfect. Fencing, riding, track and field— every sport scheduled found its facilities excellent.

Los Angeles had even built a splendid Olympic Village to accommodate the two thousand athletes from thirty-nine countries who had come to compete. Well, not quite *all* the athletes! Women weren't allowed in this Village, where comfortable cottages stood and dozens of chefs prepared the special foods each country's athletes were used to. Women were housed in a Los Angeles hotel.

Babe didn't care at all where she had to sleep or eat. She had more important things to think about: the 80-meter hurdles, the javelin throw, and the high jump. These were the three events she had decided to enter.

How did she do? In the hurdles she smashed both the Olympic and world records to win her first gold medal. In the javelin she again broke both records, for her second gold medal. In the high jump she tied for first place. The judges ruled against her. They said she dove over the pole instead of going feet first. They gave her second place. And Babe shook her head in wonder. Every time she had jumped the way she had always jumped—without any penalty.

Babe turned professional after the Olympic Games.

"I need the money," she said simply. And indeed she did. There were her aging parents to support, brothers and sisters to help, nieces and nephews to put through school. As far as she was concerned, she could get along on very little, but there were others to think of.

She played pro basketball. She played for a while on the bearded, all-male House of David baseball team, and once pitched an inning for the St. Louis Cardinals. She wrote a series of syndicated articles. She toured the country in billiards exhibitions. She did figure skating. And she traveled all over the

United States with her own vaudeville act: "Doing things I know how to do," she said. "Like acrobatics and playing the mouth organ."

She also decided that there was one sport left for her to conquer: golf. She saved enough money to live on—frugally—for the three years she had to stay out of competition in order to return to amateur status. She would learn the game in that time. To her surprise, Babe found that golf didn't come easily to her. She practiced every day for hours under a good coach, and then she practiced some more.

"I never just wished for something," Babe said. "I went to work to get it."

When the palms of her hands grew raw from swinging her clubs, she taped them up and went on practicing. She entered her first tournament, and lost it. She practiced harder. She entered the Texas Women's Golf Association championship. And won it. The United States Golf Association then ruled that she could not compete any longer as an amateur. So Babe turned pro again.

Then one day in 1938 Babe met George Zaharias, a smiling giant of a man, a professional wrestler with a heart as big as his biceps and gentleness in his eyes. It was love at first sight for George. It took a little longer for Babe, who had made up her mind long before that trying to belong to anybody would only turn into hurt. There was no way that this was going to be true now. George saw to that!

They were married two days before Christmas,

1938, and no one called Babe plain. Feminine from head to toe, hair softly curled, makeup perfect, figure slim, she was as beautiful as any bride who ever walked down the aisle. Maybe it was the happiness shining in her eyes that helped make her so beautiful.

Home was a cottage in southern California, kept spotless by Babe, and surrounded by thirty-five varieties of roses. She cooked Norwegian dishes her mother had taught her, and George taught her Greek ones. She managed a sportswear shop next to George's custom-tailoring establishment. She designed and made sports clothes for herself. There were so many inquiries about them that she began designing for a select clientele, who paid handsomely for her exclusive models.

During World War II national tournaments were suspended, but Babe kept on practicing, George more often than not at her side. In January 1944, again having been out of play for the required three years, she was reinstated as an amateur, and once more her name was headlined on the sports pages.

WESTERN OPEN SEMI-FINALS:
BABE ZAHARIAS WINNER.
UTAH OPEN: BABE ZAHARIAS WINNER.

And on and on it went: 1946, 1947, 1948 . . . Babe Didrikson Zaharias . . . winner, winner, winner.

A scarecrow? Not this slim, gray-green-eyed young woman in her chic sports clothes, joking from time to time with the gallery, showing golf style that

had as much grace as power, he
hovering close by, blowing smoke
show Babe the direction of the wind
perfect shot).

"She outdraws the big majority
heroes," one news columnist wrote. "Pla
women's tees, she'll equal men's par 60 perc        ᴏne
time. . . . And she's the first woman golfer to pay attention to showmanship." What a change from that
long-ago day that the spectators had laughed at her!

By 1947 Babe had won every major amateur
championship there was. Once again she turned pro.
And now Babe Didrikson Zaharias was to face the
greatest fight she had ever faced. No one but Babe and
her husband knew of the battle ahead when, in the
spring of 1953, she entered—and won—the tournament which had been named for her. Ten days later
Babe went into a hospital in Beaumont and was
operated on for cancer.

"I'll be back," she promised. Three-and-a-half
months later she was. In the withering summer heat of
Chicago she took third in the All-American. Six
months later she won $5,000 in a Miami meet. In 1954
she captured three more titles.

But the odds had piled up against Babe. She had
to return to the hospital, and this time she knew she
wasn't going to make it. Floods of letters poured in.
Flowers filled the room. Her golf clubs stood in one
corner where she could see them. And George—

ge who loved this woman with his whole heart—
kept constant vigil.

Babe died in the middle of the night with her husband at her side. She was just forty-two.

Maybe Paul Gallico, famous reporter and author, said it best when he wrote: "She was a golden person—golden of heart and spirit . . . the most splendid woman athlete of all time."

And so she was.

Superb as Babe Didrikson was, she would not have been allowed to take part in the ancient Games begun nearly three thousand years ago at Olympia in Greece. Women—and slaves—were barred from competing. They couldn't even attend as spectators. If they tried, and were discovered, the penalty was death!

Nobody knows exactly when the Olympic Games began. But in the year 776 B.C. a cook named Coroebus won the first recorded footrace and everlasting fame. From then on for almost twelve centuries the Games were held every four years. Spectators came from near and far, as many as ten thousand—a good crowd today; an enormous one then.

The Games were a five-day combination festival and athletic competition. City kings in royal robes attended; philosophers and rich merchants, humble fishermen and workmen—so long as they were "free men" they were welcome. Venders hawked food and wine. Poets wrote odes. Conjurers and acrobats performed. Feasts were held.

The Games were based on a concept of Greek philosophy called *arete*, which means excellence in every area of life: physical, intellectual, and moral. Contestants were screened by a ten-man panel of judges, and the screening was rigorous. A blot on a young man's character, some questionable act on the part of his mother or father, and that contestant was out as surely as if he had failed his physical tests. Each chosen competitor took a solemn oath that he would use no unfair practice in competition, and that he had trained assiduously for at least ten months before that year's Games.

The earliest Games featured only one athletic event: a 200-yard footrace called the *stade* (we get our word *stadium* from it). As the years went by, other events were added: wrestling, boxing, javelin, discus, chariot racing, broad jump, and the supreme test of all, the *pancratium*. This was a form of wrestling to the finish, with eye gouging the only thing barred. Contestants wrestled without any rest period until one of them could no longer continue. One famous contender named Arrachion was named the winner as he lay dead in the stadium. In the match his opponent had been strangling him. Arrachion knew he was losing consciousness. Summoning his last ounce of strength, he grasped his opponent's foot and twisted it so hard that the pain made his opponent raise his hand in a sign of defeat. At his final breath, Arrachion was named the winner. He had died rather than give up.

Winners were given great honors in the ancient Games. Most coveted was the crown of olive leaves cut with a golden sickle from a sacred tree, the symbol of all the athlete had tried for. There were other rewards: statues erected in public squares, feasts, and celebrations. And there were gifts of money from princes and wealthy merchants.

By A.D. 394, almost twelve centuries after their start, the Games had fallen into disrepute and come to an end. Young athletes were no longer willing to train; city-states hired professionals to take their places. At last the Games were abolished.

And where had women been during all these centuries? Not sitting meekly accepting the law that barred them from competition! Secretly they set up their own athletic meet called the Heraea. They were taking their lives in their hands, but that didn't stop them. They trained in secret, and every four years they slipped away to their own contests and crowned their own winners.

Fifteen centuries passed between the last of the ancient Olympics and the beginning of the modern

Games. And today's Games might never have been started if it hadn't been for a man named Baron de Coubertin. Son of a noble French family, he had a dream that nations could live in peace. He believed that if he could bring the youth of all nations together in athletic events, they would help build international understanding.

"The foundation of human morality," he wrote, "lies in mutual respect—and to respect one another it is necessary to know one another."

Baron de Coubertin became a one-man irresistible force. He talked Olympics to anyone who would listen, lined up influential backers, argued with disbelievers, raised money. He devoted his life to the reestablishment of the Olympics and all that they stood for.

And he triumphed. In 1896 the first of the modern Games was held in Athens. Seven nations sent teams. The king of Greece, with the duke of Sparta at his right, presided. And while women attended, none competed. Such an idea occurred to no one of official standing.

Nor were women athletes admitted in Paris, where the next Games were held. When the 1904 Games came around, in St. Louis, a woman was involved: Alice Roosevelt, daughter of President Teddy Roosevelt, placed a laurel wreath on the brow of the man who had been declared winner of the 26-mile-long marathon. (It turned out he'd hopped a ride for

part of the way on a horse-drawn wago\
disqualified.) There were also half a dc\
contenders; lady archers had been admit\
not have seen them centerfield, though. 1\
tucked away unobtrusively to compete wi\
other, but at least they were there!

A few women athletes began to agitate for admission to Olympic competition. Their voices were pretty well drowned out by the objectors. "Scandalous!" one paper declaimed. "The end of femininity," another stated. "Women will become abhorrently mannish!" "The ruination of the Games!" "The downfall of womanhood!" All such dire things were predicted. It took a very courageous woman to buck such opinions. Still a few kept trying.

They could have used a Donna de Varona in those days. Donna won two gold medals for her swimming prowess in Tokyo, 1964. Since her retirement as an amateur competitor she has devoted a good deal of her time and boundless energy to furthering the equal rights of women athletes.

Born in San Diego, California, in April of 1947, Donna was a waterbug almost before she was able to toddle. By age three she was paddling about in nearby Mission Bay with her brother and sister, completely confident. It was hard to get her to come out of the water.

The family moved to a pleasant home in a San Francisco suburb when she was seven, and Donna liked

.. just fine. There were plenty of pools and beaches nearby to keep her happy. Her dad, a fine athlete himself and the first man at the University of California to be on the championship crew and the Rosebowl championship football team (he played tackle) in the same year, recognized Donna's talent and took her in hand.

"In fact," says blonde, hazel-eyed Donna, "he coached me in everything from swimming to piano!"

Most people called her "Fishie," but he called her "Honey Bear," and when she entered her first real race at nine, he was there. It was a big meet, a western championship. Donna entered the 50-meter freestyle for ten- to twelve-year-olds. There were forty other competitors entered in the same race.

Her elimination race came early in the morning. Donna qualified. Now came an endless wait. One race after another was held. Donna and the other competitors waited. Nobody knew when their race might be called, and they couldn't have lunch, because they couldn't go into the water too soon after eating. So Donna fidgeted and waited, tried to relax, watched the other swimmers as they thrashed down the pool. Dinnertime came. Donna could only look hungrily at other people's hamburgers and feel her mouth water.

Finally, just past seven o'clock, her race was called. She was a tired, hungry little girl and, by this time, jittery. She took her place beside the others. And then she false started. Five more times that race was called, and five more times Donna went into the water before the gun sounded. Once she swam the whole length of the pool before she realized no one else was swimming.

Almost anybody else might have given up at this point, but not Donna. She squared her small jaw, climbed back into place. This time she didn't beat the gun. She didn't beat any other little girl swimmer, either. She tied for last place.

It was a sad ending to a day that had begun so brightly. She cried a little—it's hard not to at nine.

But the loss of her first big race wasn't the end of her determination. Rather, as faced losses can do, it added impetus to her efforts. She had the will to win, and that makes a difference.

A well-known California coach, Teiiko Ruuska, had seen Donna race and he asked her parents to let her train with him.

"I think she can make the Olympics—if she will work."

Would she! She'd work her head off for a chance like that. And she pretty nearly did. There were hours of working out with other swimmers, hours of private training. Meets to attend. At ten she won her first medal. And got her picture in the papers.

"A good-looking kid," her dad boasted, and her chest swelled proudly.

Things weren't going too well under Coach

Ruuska at this point. For one thing, his daughter was in the same training group, and had made the best records. Now Donna was beating her, which made things a little uncomfortable. Donna didn't want to quit, that was for sure. She had her sights already set on the Olympics. She was in a bit of a quandary.

Then came an offer from coach George Haines. "Come and train under me at the Santa Clara Swim Club."

Coach Haines was known as the champion-maker. He was good. And he was tough. He trained winners, and he only wanted swimmers dedicated enough to become champions. Donna qualified.

Five hours a day. Six hours. Up at 5:30. Breakfast. Workout. School. Workout. Supper. Off to bed at 9:00. She pulled on rubber tubes to strengthen her arms and her shoulder muscles. She held onto a kickboard, making her legs do all the work for her. She swam in her sweatsuit with her ankles tied together, a bucket tied to them to act as a drag. She did dry-land exercises.

And she won medals. One after another. At the Outdoor Championship Meet in Indianapolis she took first in the 400-meter medley, third in the freestyle, and third and fourth in other races. Magazines and newspapers sat up and took notice. Who was this kid, suddenly winning all kinds of big races? Flashbulbs popped and camera shutters clicked.

"Don't let it go to your head," Coach Haines

growled. "There's a lot of competition out there, waiting like sharks."

Almost unbelievably soon the 1960 Olympic Games at Rome rolled around. Donna de Varona, aged thirteen, was going!

It was an unforgettable experience. A beautiful new stadium. The Villagio Olympico, where nearly six thousand athletes from eighty-four countries stayed. The fabulous Olympic-sized pool. The new blue jacket, white skirt and beret, the red shoulder bag—uniforms for the United States teams. Donna wore hers proudly in the dramatic opening ceremonies.

Her specialty, the 400-meter medley she had come all these miles to compete in, was eliminated from the schedule. That race is the toughest of all—like the decathlon in track and field. You must swim four laps, using a different stroke for each: freestyle, butterfly, breast stroke, and backstroke. You've got to be tops in all of them if you want to win. And little Donna de Varona was. But there was no race for her to enter that year.

Four years later the Olympics would be in Tokyo. Donna went home to train for it. At Rome she had been the youngest member of the American team; in Tokyo she'd be seventeen, in the senior-citizen bracket as girl swimmers go. This didn't daunt her in the least. She already had four hundred trophies, and she had no intention of stopping until she had added an Olympic medal. She intensified her training to eight hundred miles a year and budgeted her time so well that she kept up a B average in high school and led a lively social life. Donna de Varona didn't want to miss anything.

When the 1964 Tokyo Games opened, Donna was ready. And if the opening ceremonies in Rome had thrilled her, Tokyo's made her weep with emotion. The National Stadium in Meiji Shrine Outer Gardens was jammed. Jet planes drew the five interlocking circles, symbol of the Olympics, in the sky with colored smoke. The flags of the ninety-four competing nations rose in unison on poles set atop the ramparts as massed bands played the Olympic Overture. Then there was silence, and suddenly the stadium was filled with the plaintive melody of hundreds of temple bells, eerily beautiful. Emperor Hirohito and his court were in the royal box. Donna marched in the parade of nations.

Then came the most dramatic moment of every Olympics: the arrival of the torch. Always kindled at Olympia in Greece, the torch is carried by thousands of relay runners who pass it from hand to hand until the site of the Games is reached, there to light the Olympic Flame. When they must cross a sea or an ocean, they take a plane or a boat. The final runner is always from the host country. And this year the runner carrying the torch for the final lap was a boy born near Hiroshima the day the atomic bomb was dropped.

A breathless silence fell over the stadium as he

entered, and then as he ran toward the carpeted stairway leading to the top of the stadium, cheers mounted with his every step. Feather-light, he ran up the stairs and stood for a moment outlined against the sky, the torch held high. Then he plunged it into the huge brazier and the Flame leaped to life, there to burn until the Tokyo Games were over.

And at those Games, Donna de Varona won not just one gold medal, but two: the gold as a member of the 400-meter freestyle relay team, the individual gold for the tough 400-meter medley. That year she was named the outstanding female athlete in the world by two of the largest newspaper syndicates, Associated Press and United Press International. By the time she retired the following year she had set eighteen world swimming records.

"Retired" is not exactly the right word for Miss de Varona! As soon as she graduated from UCLA she headed for New York and a career as a television sportscaster—a field which was considered clearly marked "For Men Only." Donna didn't let that bother her. She now works full time for NBC, covering all kinds of sports events and interviewing famous athletes.

Donna has also involved herself very thoroughly in the cause of amateur athletes in general, and women athletes in particular. In 1975, she was a member of President Ford's Commission on Olympic Sports. "The finest study ever done on amateur sports," she says. She was the driving force behind the Amateur Sports Act, lobbying in Washington and campaigning for Title IX, a bill designed to give women equality in sports. Both have been passed.

"They give athletes a voice in their own sports," she says. "It will help with facilities and help those who haven't enough money to train for the Olympics."

She is a trustee of the Women's Sports Foundation, which encourages women's participation in sports, runs workshops, provides opportunities, and distributes information to those interested. She worked with Vice-President Hubert Humphrey and with Bing Crosby, both supporters of programs for young athletes; she helped the Kennedy family with their Olympics for the Handicapped. And she serves on the United States Olympic Committee.

What does she do in her spare time! Well, there's her apartment in New York City to keep up, entertaining to do, dates. She works out three or four times a week, swimming, jogging, and weight lifting. She does some writing; keeps speaking engagements.

Anything else? "Oh, yes," she says. "I watch my diet. I love rich foods and have to battle to keep away from them."

Considering her victories in everything else, no one worries too much about Donna de Varona not winning this one.

They called her "Little Miss Poker Face." They also called her "Queen Helen." Both titles fit her.

Her name was Helen Wills, and if there had been an organization to advance women's sports in her day, Helen might have been president. She was beautiful, regal, ambitious, imperious, and efficient. In a starched white dress, wearing the green-and-white eye shade that was her trademark, it took her less than half an hour to defeat her opponent and win the 1924 Olympic tennis championship on the courts of Paris. She had already won every other trophy, medal, and honor there was to win. She was just nineteen, and a star in her own right.

In those days tennis was an Olympic sport, though it isn't today. Through the London Games of 1908, through those in Stockholm in 1912 and Antwerp in 1920 (World War I knocked out the 1916 Games), women had been inching their way toward admittance. Women swimmers had appeared in "daring" costumes, puff-sleeved and full-skirted; long stockings covering what were generally known as "extremities" (the word "legs" was indelicate). Some women equestriennes had appeared. A few stout-hearted women fencers had performed, and a handful of archery experts.

But up until the twenties, when flappers bobbed their hair, kicked up their heels in the Charleston, and painted "Cupid's bows" on their lips, you would have been hard put to find any newspaper coverage of women in the Olympics. A few long-forgotten names, perhaps, in small print. Or scathing editorials about the folly of women who dared to participate in men's affairs!

But they were daring more and more, and Helen Wills was one whose name began to make headlines:
LITTLE MISS POKER FACE WINS PACIFIC
COAST JUNIOR GIRLS' CHAMPIONSHIP
(she was fifteen then).
QUEEN HELEN TAKES NATIONAL TITLE.
GIRL PRODIGY TAKES
WOMEN'S NATIONAL SINGLES.
Helen was not only winning; she was capturing

the attention of both press and public right over the heads of male competitors. And by leaping to fame in a "man's world" she brought a new dimension to the world of sports.

She was born in Berkeley, California, in 1905. Her father was a prominent doctor, and wealthy. As an only child, Helen never had to want for anything—except, perhaps, for friends. Papa Wills, who believed in outdoor exercise, good food, and male supremacy, made the rules and picked Helen's playmates. Not every little girl was welcome in Helen's home.

She and her mother were chums. They shared confidences, "women's work" around the house, maybe wishful dreams about more feminine freedom. Her mother was a gifted artist (painting was considered "ladylike") and Helen inherited her talent. Many of her solitary hours were spent painting. Here her imagination took flight and her vulnerable side, seldom shown in public, was visible.

When she was still in pigtails, her silky brown braids tied with big taffeta bows, her father gave her a tennis racket. The game was just becoming fashionable then and he no doubt imagined her playing ladylike games on society club courts. But Helen was soon beating the bloomers off her little girlfriend opponents. And equally soon they began to vanish. It was no fun being beaten consistently. Young Helen took on the boys. Soon they vanished, too.

Helen's father took note. He was proud of his daughter and liked her to excel. He saw to it that she had good coaching at the fashionable Berkeley Tennis Club and from then on there was no stopping her. Her coach found her a methodical young lady (she was then thirteen), able to concentrate, willing to practice hours on end. Some days she would repeat a single stroke a thousand times.

"I want it *right,*" she'd say firmly.

She would spend hours firing a tennis ball across the net to hit a white handkerchief placed in the opposite court. She returned balls endlessly, watching each stroke and calculating its effectiveness. And she began winning tournament after tournament.

She won seven United States singles titles between 1923 and 1931, and shared in four doubles crowns. She won the Olympic title. She played in ten Wightman Cup singles, winning eighteen games, losing only two. She became the idol of the American public—the best woman tennis player in the United States. Headlines shouted her name, people cheered her wherever she went. She was Queen Helen, and she dined with famous writers and artists, was presented to King Gustave of Sweden and the queen of England.

There was another tennis queen in those days: vivacious, witty, chic—and sometimes snooty—Suzanne Lenglen of France, the European champion. Inevitably, a match was scheduled between Suzanne and Helen. The date set was February 16, 1928.

"I have beaten everyone except Helen Wills," Suzanne said, making a pretty face at the clustering reporters, "and she has beaten everyone but me. Now we will see."

The press went wild. They flocked to the French resort of Cannes where the match was to take place. Suzanne was very much at home in that resort. Her admirers were legion. Photographers adored her and couldn't take enough pictures. Suzanne flirted her way through it all, decked out in the most fashionable clothes and managing to make her opponent look uncomfortably provincial. It shook Helen, though she tried not to let it.

On the court Mademoiselle Lenglen was anything but a frothy flirt. She played dazzling tennis, fought hard, never giving an inch. And she took the match from Helen 6–3, 8–6. It was a rough defeat for Little Miss Poker Face.

After Cannes, Helen found herself locked in deadly battle with another champion, the great Helen Jacobs. Their first match initiated one of the most famous sports feuds ever to capture the attention of the nation. First Helen Wills took a match, then Helen Jacobs, with the press wringing every ounce of drama possible out of the contest. The battle seesawed back and forth until one day at Forest Hills. Helen Jacobs was challenging Helen Wills. Wills was defending her championship.

Unknown to the press and the public, Queen

Helen had suffered a back injury earlier in the season. It was like her to have kept that injury secret—she was not one who could ever ask favors or look for sympathy. Lonely in spite of her popularity, she kept personal problems to herself.

She went onto the court aware of the pain she was suffering and determined to put down her rival. The match began. Miss Jacobs played steadily and won the first set 8–6. Helen battled back and took the next set 6–3. Her fans cheered wildly, sure that now they would see their favorite demolish Miss Jacobs.

Pain was shooting into Helen's shoulders and down her legs like sharp-tipped arrows. Her play faltered and her fans groaned. Miss Jacobs jumped into a 3–0 lead. The match seemed to be hers. Then a startling thing happened. As Miss Jacobs was about to serve, Helen Wills turned and walked carefully to the umpire. She spoke a few words to him, leaned down and picked up her soft blue sweater—and walked off the court!

The crowd sat stunned. It looked as though she had defaulted rather than be defeated in play. Miss Jacobs was declared the winner, but it was a hollow victory for her. Far more important would have been the on-court championship.

Ignorant of the facts, the press turned on Helen Wills in fury. They called her a poor sport, a traitor to all the game stood for.

QUEEN AFRAID TO FACE CHALLENGE!

the headlines shouted.

HELEN WILLS QUITS! ALL WASHED UP!

Helen suffered the unfair attacks in silence. She returned to California and entered a hospital. It was only then that the press learned of her injury—and that it was a serious spinal one. They retracted their statements and Helen never let anyone know how badly they'd hurt her. She locked that pain inside.

She did not play for the rest of that year, nor all of the next one. And the papers hinted that she would never play again. Helen knew better. She began practicing, working, rebuilding her skills. The biggest tournament of them all was coming up: Wimbledon in England.

"I'm going to play," Helen said quietly. "And I'm going to win." The press was skeptical. The fans she still had were hopeful.

She sailed for England, and the tournament began. Things didn't go well for her. She'd been out of competition tennis for two years. She looked shaky on the court. But she had kept her technical know-how, and she managed to stay alive. And now the press was behind her again. She was a fighter! She was their Helen!

The final matches came. And Helen Wills faced—Helen Jacobs!

Tension in the stands ran high. Could she do it? Could she come back? Or would the queen at last lose her throne?

Miss Jacobs took the lead. She still held that lead when the seventh game came up, and she won it. The eighth game went to deuce. Miss Jacobs had the advantage. She drove deep into Helen's court, forcing Helen into a weak return. It should have been an easy kill for Miss Jacobs. But then something happened! Jacobs's return went into the net! She had lost the advantage.

Now Helen Wills moved in. With the cool, clear, ruthless moves of a champion, she mowed her opponent down. She won the match. She won the Wimbledon championship. She had done what she said she would. She had kept the promise she'd made to herself.

Queen Helen . . . Little Miss Poker Face . . . One of the first women to break the men-only barrier. Proud. Often misunderstood. Frequently lonely. She was a champion and she led the way for many women athletes who would follow her.

Babe Didrikson displays a golf trophy, circa 1935. Babe excelled in every sport she tried, but it was her performance in track and field that won her two gold medals at the Los Angeles Olympics of 1932.

Helen Wills (right) looks unhappy after being defeated by Suzanne Lenglen of France at their famous tennis match in Cannes, 1926. Helen had won two gold medals for the U.S. two years before, when tennis was still an Olympic sport.

Donna de Varona tears
through the butterfly lap
of the individual medley
to win the National AAU
Championship in 1964.
Later that same year,
Donna, at age seventeen,
won two gold medals at
the Tokyo Olympics.

Donna today as a televi-
sion sportscaster.

A formal portrait of Gertrude Ederle, who captured the gold for swimming in 1924 and who, in 1926, became the first woman to swim the English Channel.

Norwegian Sonja Henie, at age
eleven, at the Winter Games in
Chamonix, 1924. She placed
last in figure skating that year,
but the gold medal was hers in
1928, 1932, and 1936.

Sonja as a professional. She had
her own ice show and starred in
numerous Hollywood movies.

Tenley Albright, twice World Champion, earned the silver medal at Oslo in 1952 and the gold at Cortina, Italy, in 1956.

Carol Heiss, Tenley's "friendly rival," won the silver medal at Cortina, wrested the World Championship that same year, and finally got her gold in the Squaw Valley, California, Games in 1960.

Peggy Fleming turned pro after winning the gold medal in Grenoble in 1968 and holding the World Championship for three years. Here, in an ice show, she displays the grace of a ballerina.

Speed skater Sheila Young rockets into first place in the 500-meter race at Innsbruck in 1976, earning a gold medal and setting a new Olympic record.

Galina Zybina of the U.S.S.R. at Helsinki, 1952. Galina won her gold medal in the shotput, and also set a new world's record.

Wilma Rudolph, the "Black Gazelle," dashes into first place in the Rome Games in 1960, where she became the first American woman to win three gold medals for running.

Wilma today.

# IV

In 1924, the year Queen Helen won her Olympic championship, a sturdy, brown-eyed seventeen-year-old won a gold medal at the same Paris Games and went on to become the first woman swimming celebrity in history. Her name was Gertrude Ederle. Everyone called her Trudy.

She didn't burst into print from her Paris achievement. Headlines that year were captured by a distance runner named Paavo Nurmi, the Flying Finn, who astonished the world by doing what no other man had ever done: he won the 1500- and 5000-meter races in the same afternoon, topping it off the next day by successfully taking the 10,000-meter cross-country run.

Trudy would have been astonished if anybody *had* written about her or her winning team, even though they helped rack up the 255 points that made the United States the highest scorer. (Technically, there are no championship nations in the Olympics, only individual winners; but inevitably scores are added up, though Coubertin would have disapproved strenuously.) Even when women competitors did win, they were barely mentioned.

Trudy was born in a big, old-fashioned house in New York City's Upper West Side, next door to the prospering butcher shop her father owned. It was a fun-loving household, fond of games and big company dinners, the table laden with Mama's hearty German-American cooking: stuffed roast goose, thick juicy pork chops, good potato pancakes, rich Black Forest chocolate cake. Needless to say, Trudy was as plump as she was cheerful.

There were five little brothers and sisters to help keep things lively, and Mama Ederle raised them all in a no-nonsense fashion. Chores were done on time and done well—or done over. The boys stoked the coal-burning furnace and carried out the ashes; the girls cooked and sewed, and at an early age Trudy made all of her own clothes, as well as those of her smaller sisters.

"Nobody is special around here!" Mama Ederle said. "Everyone is a member of the family and pulls his own weight."

The family owned a summer cottage in Highland, New Jersey, and it was there Trudy learned to swim. Papa tied a rope around her waist and tossed her into the water, and it was sink or swim. Of course, if she didn't kick and paddle, there was always the rope to drag her out.

Trudy took to the water like a baby seal, and in no time at all she was swimming endlessly up and down, sturdy legs churning and strong arms stroking. By the age of ten she could outlast and outdistance everyone in the place.

Some years before, a young woman named Annette Kellerman, a polio victim, had taken up swimming to strengthen her weakened muscles. It took her no time at all to figure out that the cumbersome woolen "bathing dresses" still in vogue were no help to her recovery. She devised a one-piece suit, and when she became expert and her figure very beautiful, she launched herself into vaudeville, giving swimming exhibitions. The country survived the shock, and soon all young women were taking to the water in their "Annette Kellermans," as the bathing suits were called. Swimming quickly became a favorite women's sport.

In 1917, a group of these modern young swimmers formed an organization called the Women's Swimming Association, working out in a small pool on the Lower East Side of New York, properly chaperoned by an older woman and coached by an expert, L. B. de Handley. Many swimming stars were developed at this club.

When she was thirteen, Trudy was invited to join. It was a great honor for a little girl. Trudy was ecstatic and her family was proud of her, though her mother declared that no special exercises beyond swimming were needed to make a champion. "A girl who wants to develop her arm and shoulder muscles should do what Trudy has to do: beat heavy carpets and use a broom. Making beds will develop the muscles you need, too, if you put your mind to it and don't poke about."

Whether it was housework or coaching that did the trick, it was soon evident that Trudy's forte was in long-distance swimming. At fourteen she won the 3.5-mile International Race in New York Bay, beating fifty-one competitors, all better known than she. In the next three years she broke five world distance records and competed against the Hawaiians, who were considered the best in the world, and defeated them. In all she held five national records and ten world records. Plus the most coveted of all awards: the Olympic gold.

Then she decided to do something no other woman—and very few men—had ever done: swim the English Channel. The world was agog. She must have lost her mind! Whatever induced her to think up such a wild scheme? It was ridiculous!

"I think I can do it," Trudy said, wide brown eyes looking straight at the reporters. "I'm going to try, anyway."

Her reason for trying was totally unselfish. If she

could do this never-before-tried thing, she would bring a lot of notice to the club she belonged to. It would show what they were trying to do. It would help them. And to young Trudy Ederle, that was what mattered.

The Women's Swimming Association put together what money it could—and that wasn't much —to pay her expenses. On August 18, 1925, she went into the cold, turbulent Channel off the coast of France and headed toward England, twenty-three miles away. She had never swum this far in her life, and she had never had to swim in such angry waters. She battled for seventeen miles. With only six more to go, a huge wave engulfed her. Her trainer thought she was drowning. Frantically he ordered an assistant to jump in and save her.

"Don't touch her!" someone cried. "It will disqualify her!"

But the assistant was already at Trudy's side, forcing her, fighting and crying, into the boat. "I could have made it!" she wept. "I could have finished!"

Maybe the trainer was right; maybe Trudy was. At any rate, this Channel attempt ended in defeat. It came close to writing the finish line to Trudy Ederle's try at the "impossible" swim. The association had no more money to back her. Her papa couldn't swing it himself, much as he believed in Trudy's ability. Then, out of the blue, help arrived. Colonel Patterson, publisher of the *News* and *Chicago Tribune* syndicate, stepped in to back her, in return for her exclusive story if she made it.

A contract was drawn up. Trudy was guaranteed her expenses, a small salary, and, if successful, a bonus. Accepting that contract was tough for her. It meant giving up her amateur status. No more Olympics. No more national or international meets representing her club. None of these things she had come to love.

She signed the contract and went to Cap Gris Nez in France to train. Her older sister Margaret, her papa, her coach, and over a dozen eager reporters went with her.

Her swim began at 7:09 A.M. August 6, 1926, when she stepped into the cold, sullen, choppy waters of the Channel. She had cut her bathing suit in half, fashioning the first two-piece suit in existence, to expedite her swimming. She wore a close-fitting red bathing cap, snug goggles to keep salt water out of her eyes, and a heavy coating of sheep's grease all over her body to ward off the cold. Only five men of all those who had tried had completed this soul-testing swim. Wall Street gamblers were betting two to one that she would fail. Millions of people were rooting for her, and they stayed glued to their radios, not wanting to miss a stroke.

"I want two things," Trudy shouted as she waded into the surf. "Nobody's to pull me out! And if I make it, I get a red roadster!"

And so the swim began, with the French tug *Alsace* carrying her trainers, her father and sister, and a jazz band to keep up her spirits. Another boat full of reporters followed.

The sea was choppy. Trudy's red cap frequently disappeared beneath the waves. At ten o'clock it began to rain, and the sea grew rougher. A good many reporters were seasick. Trudy plowed on. At noon she had some chicken broth from a baby bottle dangled on a line from the side of the *Alsace.* The band played "Barney Google" and "The Star-Spangled Banner" to cheer her on. Trudy hummed to herself, and kept up her six-beat kick with metronome precision. The miles went by.

Suddenly a line squall came up, whipping the Channel into a boiling cauldron. It was impossible! Nobody could make it!

"You've got to come out!" her anxious trainer shouted.

"What for?" Trudy shouted back, and asked for another of the sugar lumps she had been sucking for quick energy.

Her lips and mouth were swollen from the salt water. The waves seemed bent on destroying her. Still she kept going. People in the accompanying boats wrote signs to encourage her and held them over the sides. The band stepped up its music. Trudy kept going.

She'd been in the water twelve hours now, and the English coast was only five miles farther on. And now Trudy struck the wicked waves. She would gain one yard and be battered back two. Close as the shore was, there seemed no possible way for this indomitable girl to make it!

"You *must* come out!" the trainer ordered. "Now, Trudy! *Now!*"

"I'm doing the swimming!" she shouted back through her swollen lips. "I'll decide when I come out!"

Two hours later, Trudy Ederle struggled out of the sea onto the English coast, her hands clasped above her head in a sign of victory. Thousands of people were gathered there to greet her, and they cheered themselves hoarse. Dozens of bonfires had been lit. Band music was playing. The news was flashed around the world by radio. The whole world was at her feet.

The next morning one of the big London papers came out with an editorial saying that women must withdraw from competitive athletics, and that it was futile for them to compete. The paper said that they would remain forever inferior to men.... The editorial had been set in print the night before Trudy's astonishing victory. It was too late to stop it. So on the day Trudy beat the fastest Channel-crossing time any man had ever made by a full two hours, the editorial was printed. No doubt the editors ate their words with suitable humility.

She went home to a heroine's welcome. As her ship made its way into New York Harbor, the whistle cord on every steamship was tied down, making a riot of sound. Fireboats sprayed water high into the air. Airplanes buzzed overhead. The welcoming committee boasted the city's highest dignitaries. A motorcade started triumphantly from lower Broadway with a bewildered but happy Trudy perched in the back of an open car. Crowds jammed the streets, and as the cavalcade inched its way uptown, a paper blizzard rained down on her. From every skyscraper's windows, streamers of ticker tape and snowstorms of torn paper drifted down. It was the first of New York's now famous ticker-tape welcome-home demonstrations for returning victors. And it was for Trudy.

She was given the keys to the city, a celebrity-studded banquet—and the red roadster she had wanted. Fabulous offers for endorsements, appearances, tours poured in. But Trudy Ederle, the simple, trusting, unspoiled girl, didn't know how to cope with this sudden overwhelming fame. Instead of turning to an experienced manager, she let "friends" handle her business, and they frittered her chances away, letting the big offers slip through their fingers, sending her out eventually on a grueling tour of exhibitions, many in small towns. Exhaustion took its toll. Rapidly increasing deafness, brought on by the fearful buffeting she had taken in the sea, added to the intolerable strain. Trudy suffered a nervous breakdown.

The years that followed were not generous to Trudy Ederle. Her deafness became complete. In 1933, she fell down a flight of stairs, injuring her back so badly that she was in a body cast for four years. Doctors said she would never swim again—perhaps not even walk. But Trudy did both, though never without pain. In 1939 she swam in the World's Fair Aquacade—which she said was harder than crossing the Channel.

There were joys, though, in these later years. Trudy designed a swimming pool with safety devices for children. President Eisenhower appointed her to his Citizens Advisory Committee on the Fitness of American Youth. Her name, along with Babe Didrikson's, was added to the International Women's Hall of Fame. And perhaps for the greatest joy of all, Trudy taught deaf children to swim. The pleasure shining in their faces was the only reward this champion asked.

V

In 1924, the year both Trudy Ederle and Helen Wills
won their gold medals, the first Winter Olympics were
held in January at Chamonix, France, a beautiful,
snowbound Alpine resort that looks like a Christmas
picture postcard.

There had been a good deal of agitation for a
Winter Olympics for some time. Figure skating had
been a popular sport since before the turn of the cen-
tury—popular not just with men but with women. It
had been included in the Summer Games on indoor
rinks.

By 1924, pressure for Winter Games was too

strong to resist. They were officially scheduled. There were skiing, bobsledding, speed skating, and ice hockey, as well as figure skating, the only event open to women.

A tiny, dimpled, eleven-year-old Norwegian girl won the hearts of every spectator. She looked like a little doll as she glided onto the rink in her fur-trimmed costume, golden curls dancing, silver skates flashing. As she pirouetted and whirled through intricate steps, the charmed spectators applauded every move she made. Her name was Sonja Henie, and although she did not place in the Winter Games at Chamonix (in fact, she came in last), her name was to be in headlines for many years to come.

Sonja was born in Oslo on April 8, 1912. It should have been a warm, springlike day, but instead a wild snowstorm swept the countryside, piling up along hedgerows and dressing every tree with ermine.

"Maybe it was foretelling my career," Sonja later said.

She began dancing almost as soon as she could walk. She loved to dress up in her mother's clothes and put on shows where she was ticket-maker and -taker, chair arranger, musical director (records on a shiny-horned Gramophone)—and star. Mama and Papa were indulgent audiences, though big brother Leif was known to sneak out when the chance came along.

Sonja's parents were wealthy. Mr. Henie was a prominent furrier whose business took him all over the world. He was the proud possessor of the first auto in Oslo, and loved driving as much as he did sports. A world championship bicyclist, he had won 160 medals and trophies of all kinds, including some for skiing and speed skating. The family owned a handsome hunting lodge in Geilo, a mountain village famous for winter sports. Everyone skied—including four-year-old Sonja, who raced after her brother in a desperate attempt to win—one thing that even she didn't manage.

By this time she was taking ballet lessons. Everyone, including Sonja, whose idol was the world-renowned dancer Pavlova, was convinced that this was where her future lay. And well it might have been. But for one thing: brother Leif owned ice skates. *He* got to go skating at wonderful Frogner Stadium whenever he wanted to. Sonja was green with jealousy.

"Papa, *I* want skates!" she demanded imperiously.

"You're too young," Papa told her.

"And you have your dancing," her mother reminded her.

Certainly, Sonja didn't want to give that up. But she didn't want to stay home when Leif took off, either, and she kept up her pleading. Finally when she was six her parents capitulated. She got her skates.

Leif wasn't exactly overjoyed to have a small sister tagging after him, and he did his best to evade her, but Sonja was usually too quick for him, and there she'd be, trotting along after him, stocking cap askew and mittens dangling, a smile of pure satisfaction on her rosy face.

She had expected that ice skating would be as easy as dancing, and she was outraged and dumbfounded when time after time she plopped to the ice on her round little bottom. Her big brother took pity on her and showed her first how to fall ("You've got to sag into it—don't stay rigid") and then how to skate.

From the very first, Sonja adored skating. At the stadium there was a special section roped off for experts and Sonja was soon hanging around the edges of it, watching like a hawk, then trying to copy the intricate spins and jumps. A teacher noticed her, invited her into the sacrosanct section, gave her instructions—and from that moment on, Sonja Henie's future was decided.

At seven, she entered her first competition and won a silver paper cutter with a mother-of-pearl handle. She thought it the most beautiful thing she had ever seen, and she kept it always. In later years when she felt nervous or under stress, she'd take out the paper cutter, smooth its iridescent handle with her fingers, sleep with it under her pillow. It was her good-luck charm.

When she was eight, Sonja entered the Norwegian Junior Class C competition and won easily. She was taking professional skating lessons as well as ballet now, practicing many long hours. Because it was hard to keep up at a regular school, she had a private tutor.

She went to London to study dancing under the famous Russian ballerina, Karsavina. She trained under the best of skating instructors. Fortunately her parents could afford all of these extras and equally fortunately they both encouraged her and kept her from letting all the applause go to her head.

At ten, a year before entering the Olympics, Sonja was entered in the Norwegian National Women's Figure Skating Competition. A furor arose. She was too young—"an out-of-place baby," critics insisted. Efforts were made to have her barred. The efforts failed. Sonja didn't. She took the championship.

She followed this by winning the Scandinavian National Championship, and at thirteen she won the first of ten World Figure Skating Championships that were to be hers. Norway's Queen Maud and King Haakon were in the royal box that day and, after winning, little Sonja was presented to them. It was an enormous thrill for such a small girl. From that day on, before many of her competitions, a huge bouquet of pink carnations would arrive from the king and queen to wish her well.

Sonja's first presentation to Queen Mary of England was not quite so successful. Graciously the queen congratulated Sonja and expressed an interest in ice skating herself. Doubtfully, little Sonja eyed the queen's ample figure.

"Perhaps your Majesty might try roller skating," she suggested.

There was a long pause, and then the queen said tactfully: "I will think about that." For a long time after that Sonja's cheeks burned when she thought of her faux pas.

The 1928 Winter Olympics, to be held at St. Moritz, Switzerland, were coming up. Sonja was determined to win a gold medal. She was working her hardest.

Olympic figure skating is divided into two parts: the compulsory school figures and free skating. School figures are all part of the figure 8—and there are over sixty that can be done using the exact loops and brackets and counters, as the strokes are called. Each tracing the skates make on the ice must fall exactly over the previous line if it is to count. No skater knows exactly which figures he or she will be called on to perform. A champion must be perfect in all of them because they count heavily toward winning.

In free skating, competitors can do the loops, spins, and jumps they choose, putting them together to make a pleasing performance, and one that's as difficult as they can manage. It must be set to music and last four minutes.

Up until 1928, free-skating performances had been highly skilled but rather stiff looking. Sonja had other ideas. She was going to work the required moves into a ballet. No one had ever done this before.

She worked tirelessly with choreographers and musicians. "I'm going to be the first Pavlova on ice!"

she declared. And she was. Judges and spectators alike found her performance enchanting. She won her gold medal, and cried from happiness. Since that day in 1928, all competitors have followed Sonja's idea of blending skating and dance in their free exhibitions.

Life for Sonja turned into a dizzying whirl of competition and exhibitions following her win at St. Moritz. There were European and world championships to defend—and win. She was in great demand for exhibitions, all for some cause or charity. She was not paid, of course. That would have forfeited her amateur status.

When she was seventeen she made her first trip to America, to defend and win her fourth World Championship. Americans loved her. Everywhere she went, autograph seekers and news photographers followed her. More than fifteen thousand people jammed into Madison Square Garden, in New York, to see her star in a charity ice carnival called "The Land of the Midnight Sun"—with over a hundred skaters taking part. Sonja's appearance brought the house down. She followed this triumph with a tour of American and Canadian cities and everywhere she went she was besieged by fans, who sometimes tore off bits of her clothing for keepsakes.

Sonja was both elated and exhausted when it was over. Rest was about the only thing she wanted at the moment. But a request came from Queen Mary and King George V of England to appear at a charity exhibition in London. She could not refuse, and she never skated better. Then, at last, she went home to rest.

Offers to turn pro poured in. Hollywood movie producers courted her. Sonja said no. She won her sixth World Championship. She won her second gold medal at the 1932 Winter Games at Lake Placid in New York State. Her father gave her a brand-new roadster.

That summer Sonja entered an amateur three-day cross-country auto race—"just for fun." She came in second. Afterwards, her brother complained every time he had to ride with her. She drove too fast.

The terrific pace Sonja had to keep up began to tell. She took a fall in an exhibition in St. Moritz, and the rumor started: Sonja Henie is through.

"It's harder to stay on top than to get there," she said ruefully.

She had been in national, world, and Olympic competition for many years now, and she hadn't been beaten. She knew she couldn't go on forever. Younger skaters were coming up—and they were good!

"I want to round out the decade," Sonja said. "And then I'll retire."

Could she possibly win a third Olympic gold medal? Graceful, accomplished Maribel Vinson from the United States would be competing, and she was an inspired free skater. Cecilia Colledge of Great Britain was expert. Both were threats.

The 1936 Winter Games were held at Garmisch-

Partenkirchen, a little Bavarian village snuggled between Alpine peaks with small houses clinging to their sides. The competitions began.

Sonja took a very small lead in the school figures, with Cecilia close behind. She knew her title depended on her free-skating exhibition. Her performance was scheduled as the last event of the last night. The waiting was almost unbearable. She stayed in her room, trying to rest, one hand closed around the handle of her good-luck piece.

Then it was time. From her window she could see the glare of lights in the stadium. She knew that 200,-000 people were packed into the stands waiting to see whether she would win or lose.

She went to the rink entrance. Her music began. She skated into the spotlights in her snow-white costume. People held their breath as she spun and leaped and glided from one intricate move to another. She had never been better, and four minutes later cheers rose from the stadium. Sonja Henie had won her third gold medal!

Now a whole new life began for Sonja. She had received dozens of professional offers in the past year or two. None, she felt, was right for her. She was confident that there was a big place in the entertainment field for dancing on ice, and Hollywood was her goal.

The important producers disagreed. It would be fine for her to appear in skating interludes in feature pictures, they said, but a whole movie built around Sonja and her skating? "Not practical," they said.

Sonja was tiny, but determined. If Hollywood wouldn't come to her, she'd go to Hollywood. She hired the only ice-skating rink in the film center and in three grueling weeks put together a whole show, training the skaters, teaching the workmen how to put a professional finish on the ice, inviting the famous: Mary Pickford, Douglas Fairbanks, Spencer Tracy, Clark Gable, Ginger Rogers, Bette Davis, Jimmy Stewart—and, of course, the top producers of the biggest film companies. The one she wanted most was Darryl F. Zanuck, and she had people watching to see if he arrived. Nobody spotted him.

But a day later he contacted her. He had seen her show after all. Nervous but determined, Sonja went to his office. He asked her what she wanted.

"A leading role," Sonja said.

Mr. Zanuck made a rude sound. "Never!" he said.

Sonja argued. She pointed out the growing interest in her way of skating; the kind of movie that could be built around it. Zanuck grew interested, but insisted that some well-known Hollywood star should have the lead.

"Then I'll go somewhere else," Sonja said. "If I don't have the lead, the kind of picture I'm talking about can't be done."

Darryl Zanuck was not an easy man to convince,

but he was a man of vision, and the more Sonja talked, the more he saw the kind of money-making venture she had in mind. A five-year contract was signed. Sonja's first movie went into production. It was called *One in a Million.*

If Sonja had worked hard before, now the work was doubled. There were countless things she had to learn, not the least being acting; saying lines and playing scenes were quite different from skating. Fortunately she was fluent in English, so that was no problem.

She was terrified that the movie might fail. She need not have been. *One in a Million* was a smash hit. Sonja Henie was launched on her movie career.

One successful picture followed another. She was tops at the box office. She launched her own famous Ice Revue—the first of its kind—and toured in it. In 1952 when, at forty, she again starred in it, a reviewer wrote, "Her ice virtuosity is at its peak."

Sonja made millions of dollars; she made millions and millions of people happy with her wonderful talent and lavish productions. During World War II she made a tour of American Army Hospitals in Europe as a USO entertainer (she had become a U.S. citizen in 1941). She gave command performances before the crowned heads of Norway, Sweden, Belgium, and Great Britain, and one of her proudest honors came when she received the Order of St. Olav from King Haakon "in recognition of your unique contribution as a sportswoman, an artist, an interpreter of the ideals of Norway's youth, and one who has upheld the honor of the flag of Norway."

But of all the honors, of all the awards and trophies, nothing was more precious to the tiny, talented star than her pearl-handled paper cutter—and the three gold medals she won in the Olympics.

# VI

Women have appeared longer in figure skating than any other event in the Olympics. In 1908 the indomitable Madge Syers Cave of Great Britain was braving public opinion to prove her great skill on ice—by competing against men! She opened the door for skating stars who came later.

And what stars they have been! Madame Julin of Sweden, called graceful as a swan; Austrian Herma Planck-Szabo, noted for her precision; the USSR's Irina Rodnina, famous primarily for her incomparable pairs skating, three times a gold medal winner.

Blue-eyed Barbara Ann Scott, the Canadian National Champion, skated eleven miles every day just practicing her school figures. She was so beloved by her countrymen that when her father died and there wasn't enough money for her to continue the expensive training required, they contributed the money needed. Barbara Ann did them proud. She won the Women's European Figure Skating Championship and the World Championship, and then went on to take the Olympic gold at St. Moritz in 1948.

The United States has had its fair share of Olympic gold medalists—dazzling performers, every one: Peggy Fleming, Dorothy Hamill, Tenley Albright, Carol Heiss. And one who, except for one of those nightmare moments that happen to champions too, would almost certainly have won: Janet Lynn.

That moment came at the 1972 Winter Olympics in Sapporo, Japan. Janet was well into her free-skating exhibition and was performing with the grace and joy that made some people call her "Sunshine on Ice." She knew she was doing well—she could feel it. She soared through a leap, making it seem effortless, and the crowd cheered. She whirled into her flying sit-spin—and fell. She had done that spin hundreds of times without a single fall. And now, at the moment she wanted perfection the most, the inexplicable happened. Janet didn't win the Olympic gold, but in spite of her fall she took the third-place bronze medal.

Not long ago the great Dick Button, whose name is synonymous with supreme figure skating, included

Janet in his list of the top five all-time women skating champions (Sonja Henie was first).

"My definition of a great skater," he said, "is someone who not only reaches the top but leaves the sport better for having been in it." He compared Janet's skating to a poem and called her jumps "fountain sprays."

Two of America's gold medal winners were friendly rivals: Tenley Albright and Carol Heiss. Both started skating as small children, both faced and conquered tough troubles, both won gold medals: Tenley in 1956, Carol in 1960.

Tenley was born in Newton Center, Massachusetts, where her father was a doctor. When she was eight years old, her best-loved Christmas present was a pair of ice skates. Her dad made her a rink in the backyard, but it was soon evident that she was more than just another happy little girl skater, and within a year she was being coached at the Skating Club in nearby Boston.

Her progress was phenomenal, and she was just ready to start entering competitions when she fell ill. Specialists gave the dread diagnosis: polio. For a time it seemed that this must be the end of her dreams. She could walk with difficulty, she could move her arms, but her back was so weakened that doctors thought she would never be able to skate again.

But eleven-year-old Tenley was a fighter. "If I can walk, I can skate," she announced with finality.

Every other day she was taken to the hospital for physical therapy and muscle strengthening. At home she exercised hour after hour. It was no fun, but she stuck to it. Little by little her strength returned, and the day she was allowed to put on skates again was the happiest day of her life.

It was almost like starting from scratch, a discouraging business for anyone, but Tenley kept at it. She regained her skill. And before long she was entering and winning juvenile championships. It was only a step from that to traveling throughout the United States and Europe, piling title on title.

Meanwhile, back in Ozone Park near New York City, little Carol Heiss, five years younger than Tenley, was moving toward championship. Her skating had started when she was three-and-a-half, on roller skates, in the cement-floored basement of the family home. Just one year later she was on ice skates and under the tutelage of her first coach. She had been born with a very special gift: perfect balance.

It wasn't easy for the Heisses to finance all of the special lessons would-be champions need. The family was comfortably off but not wealthy (her father, who, owned a bakery shop, had learned the baker's trade as a boy in Munich). And there were Carol's younger sister and brother, Nancy and Bruce, to be considered. Their parents felt strongly that one child should not have an advantage the other two didn't, so lessons for all had to be paid for. Mama Heiss spent a great deal of her time at the ice rink chaperoning the children.

One day Carol's coach, the well-known Pierre Brunet, threw up his hands in despair. He had been trying to teach Carol a new free-skating routine, and she wasn't getting it. "She doesn't have any sense of rhythm!" he groaned.

What to do about it? The answer, of course, was piano lessons and ballet. The family budget simply wouldn't stretch far enough.

"I'll get a job," Mrs. Heiss said. But what kind of job? She had to oversee lessons, be at the rink—who could possibly employ her? Fortunately she had talent as an artist and she found a job painting designs on fabric. She could take her work to the rink. It was the perfect answer.

Kid sister Nancy was turning out to be almost as good a skater as Carol, and the two were often entered in pairs skating exhibitions and contests. They won the Middle Atlantic Ladies' Pairs championship and the same year, at Rye, New York, Carol won the Eastern Junior Ladies' title and eight-year-old Nancy, with a front tooth missing, took the Girls' crown. That was the same year that Tenley Albright won the senior title and placed third in free skating in the World Championship. A year later Tenley won the second-place silver medal at the Winter Olympics in Oslo.

Now both girls moved toward the 1956 Olympics. They met often in competition, vying with each other for the top awards. The first time was in Davos, Switzerland, where the World Championship was at stake. Tenley was the favorite. It was bitter cold. Two skaters, overcome by the sub-zero weather, had to be helped from the ice.

Carol, in red velvet, skated first, and the crowd was enchanted. Then it was Tenley's turn. Her performance began with slow, graceful ease, whirled into a fast movement, slowed again, then spun to a breathtaking finish. There was a moment of awed silence, then the stadium echoed with cheer after cheer. She had just become the first American woman ever to win a World Championship. Thirteen-year-old Carol had finished fourth, remarkable for her age.

Three weeks later both girls were competing for the North American title in Cleveland, and the next month for the Women's National Championship in Hershey, Pennsylvania. Both times, Tenley took first place, Carol second.

GREATEST SKATING DUEL OF ALL TIME! newspapers trumpeted in big black headlines. Tenley and Carol grinned. It was a duel, all right—they both wanted to win. But they'd become friends, too.

A bad skating accident kept Carol away from practice for weeks. She and Nancy had been working out together. In an unexpected turn they collided. Both girls went down, and Carol couldn't get up. Nancy's skate had slashed across her foot, cutting nearly to the bone.

Tenley had had to work her way back from crippling polio. Now Carol had to work to overcome the severe damage her foot had sustained. And like Tenley, she put every ounce of determination into it. Bit by bit she regained full use of her foot. She toiled to make up the lost hours of practice, but as the date drew nearer, she knew she couldn't be ready for the upcoming world contest.

Tenley was a pre-med student at Radcliffe now, working toward becoming a doctor like her father. Her schedule was rough. She had to keep her grades high if she were to have a chance at acceptance in a medical school, and that meant hours of study; but it never occurred to her not to defend her world title.

The meet was at Oslo in the stadium where she had won her Olympic medal, and it was thrilling to be back. She missed Carol. They'd been competing against each other so long it seemed strange to be there without her.

She had prepared a daring and beautiful free-skating exhibition, highlighted by a very difficult axel and double loop—a most difficult figure. She was skating beautifully when she fell. Not just a slip. She went completely down, flat on her bottom. She lost the championship she had won at Davos. The minute the skating competitions were over, she was out on the ice alone, doing the figure she had missed over and over, her mind already made up that she would regain her lost title.

At Carol's home there was sad news: Mrs. Heiss

had cancer. "We'll have no long faces!" she said. "That's not the way we meet things."

Mrs. Heiss had the required operation and came home, pretending that all was well. But the family knew that it was only pretense. Still, Mr. Heiss, Carol, Nancy, and young Bruce (now also a skating champion) tried to match the mother's courage.

The World Competition in Vienna was only a few weeks off. None of the family wanted Mrs. Heiss to go along with Carol as she always had—they knew it would be terribly hard for her.

"I'm going," Marie Heiss said; and because they knew how much it meant to her, no one argued.

Tenley, of course, was in Vienna for the competition and had prepared an extremely difficult exhibition that included some new leaps: a "stage loop jump" and "3s in spirals into a camel." Carol's exhibition was difficult, too, and she was perfect in it; but she knew what pain her mother was in, she was terribly worried, and it affected her performance. She was in sixth place at the end of the school figures, incredible for her, and sick at heart. She had wanted so badly to do her best—for her mother.

Tenley finished her free-skating exhibition. The scores went up. There were several 5.9s—6 is perfect.

Carol said a small prayer and forced everything out of her mind except her exhibition. She was utterly brilliant, but even that brilliance couldn't overcome her first low scores. Tenley won again, the first woman ever to lose and regain a world's title. Carol was second.

"You were terrific," she told Tenley honestly.

"So were you," Tenley said, as the two girls clasped hands.

Carol had only one goal now: to win over Tenley while her mother was still alive. Yet in the National and North American contests, again she took second.

"There are still the Olympics," Carol thought, but would there be time? Her mother's health was failing fast now. *Would there be time?*

The Winter Olympics were held at Cortina, Italy, in January 1956.

"You can watch on television," Carol said to her mother.

Marie Heiss would not accept this substitute. She was thinner now, terribly ill. There were treatments she must have, and long hot baths to ease the pain. These would not be possible if they stayed with the team. Mother and daughter took a private room in a separate hotel.

The gossip started. "The Heisses think they're too good for the rest of us! They're stuck up."

"Mama, let me tell them why we're at this hotel," Carol begged. Mrs. Heiss shook her head. "But *why?*" Carol insisted.

Marie Heiss's eyes met her daughter's. "Because I don't want pity," she said quietly. "For me—or for you." And Carol understood.

Tenley, although she didn't understand the Heisses' decision, maintained her friendship. But others didn't. Reporters were unkind. They called Carol and her mother "big shots" and wrote that they were unpopular with other competitors. Carol ignored them. There was only one thing that mattered: to do her best.

In the school figures her scores nearly matched Tenley's. Then it was time for the free-skating exhibition. Tenley gave an inspired performance. Carol skated her heart out, and afterward the newspapers called her exhibition the most daring ever skated by a woman at the Olympics.

But it only got her the second-place silver medal.

The World Championships were in a few weeks. Discouraged, worried, her mother's fragile strength failing every day, Carol put every ounce of skill and artistry she could muster into her performance. For the first time in her life she finished ahead of Tenley in the school figures. Battling back, Tenley outdid herself in the free skating. Then it was Carol's turn. Snow was falling as she skated onto the rink. And she was marvelous! When she finished, the crowd rose to its feet, giving her a standing ovation that seemed as if it would never stop.

One by one the judges held up their scores: 5.9—5.9—5.9—every single score the same! Carol Heiss had won the World Championship! Tears she had never shed in defeat spilled down her cheeks as she hugged her mother.

When she arrived home there were parades and cheering crowds, banquets and official greetings from high dignitaries. Carol smiled through them all, but her heart was heavy.

Mrs. Heiss died on October 30, 1956. Now reporters who had written so unkindly about Carol and her mother learned the truth, and perhaps were shamed. There was grief in the small home, but Papa Heiss and the children carried on as they knew Marie would have wanted them to. In her mind Carol said, I'll beat Tenley at the next Olympics, and Mama will know.

But on January 20, 1957, Carol's seventeenth birthday, Tenley Albright notified the United States Figure Skating Association that she was withdrawing from all future contests.

Carol felt stunned. She had wanted so much to have one last chance to win over her "friendly rival" in the Olympics! Yet she understood Tenley's decision. Tenley's high scholastic record at Radcliffe had earned her a place at Harvard Medical School. It was time for her to let her love of skating take second place.

Carol graduated from high school that year and accepted a scholarship at New York University. It was close to home and she was trying to run that home now, doing the cooking and cleaning, with help from Nancy and Bruce. With her college classes, her hours of practice, and the house to look after, she was a very busy young lady indeed, and a happy one. She had met Hayes Alan Jenkins, who had been the men's

World Champion for four years before he retired. They liked each other very much indeed.

She was absolutely determined to win in the 1960 Olympics. She won in the Nationals. She kept her World Championship. She took the North American title. She repeated her triumphs in 1959—with Nancy coming in second in the Nationals.

Now came the supreme test. The Olympics were held in Squaw Valley, California, a beautiful place in the heart of the Sierra Nevada mountains, nine thousand feet up. Ten million dollars were spent to change a winter wilderness into a fabulous arena for the Winter Games. Skaters and skiers from more than thirty countries were there, along with thousands of spectators.

Carol was the favorite out of the twenty-six girls entered in the figure-skating competition. It was a grueling competition that lasted four days. Every day sixteen skaters went on before Carol—a long, hard wait. Every day Carol's lead over her rivals increased.

The fourth day came. The time for the finals in the free-skating exhibition. She wore a brilliant red costume, and a small gold crown on her head. She had prepared the most difficult performance she could think of—and it was dazzling. Cheer after cheer rose from the stands as she finished. Then silence fell. People held their breath, waiting for the scoring.

The first score went up and a gasp came from the audience—5.5 for general impression, 5.6 for merit!

Very low scores! Carol was stunned. The scores of other judges went up—5.9—5.9—5.8.... And then cheers resounded and Carol Heiss wept. She had won her gold medal.

"It's for you, Mama," she whispered.

Four weeks later Carol announced her engagement to the handsome skater she'd met two years before: Hayes Alan Jenkins, now a rising young lawyer. It wasn't too much of a surprise to the press. They'd already noticed that where Carol was Hayes was apt to be close by.

Carol had another announcement to make that day. Like Sonja Henie, she was turning professional. There were TV, movie, and big ice-show offers.

"It cost my family a great deal to help make me a champion," she said. "It's time for me to pay back."

In April of that year, at St. Thomas Episcopal Church on New York's Fifth Avenue, Carol and Hayes were married. There was a wedding party afterward with a beautiful cake topped with silvery bells. Papa Heiss had made it.

"And that's the most beautiful thing about it," Carol said through misty tears. "I know Mama knows how happy I am!"

VII

Tenley Albright, bright star and Golden Girl of the Olympics, went on to become Dr. Albright with her own fine career. In later Olympics, instead of being a contestant, she was on the medical staff that cared for the newer United States champions. Carol Heiss found fulfillment in marriage, her movie career, and the fairy-book ice shows that made millions of people happy.

Two other figure-skating gold medalists have taken the professional route that both Sonja Henie and Carol took: willowy Peggy Fleming and Dorothy Hamill, whose saucy "wedge" haircut became a fashion first throughout America practically overnight.

It was at Grenoble, France, in 1968 that Peggy won her gold medal—the only one the United States captured that year.

Few Winter Olympic openings have been as glamorous as that one. Fireworks burst into bloom from the arena, jet planes overhead drew loops of colored smoke in the sky, parachutists landed on the field, and for a finale, fifty thousand perfumed paper roses released from the jets floated down on the thousands of spectators.

In the eight years since Carol Heiss had won her medal there had been only one Winter Olympics gold medalist from the United States: Richard McDermott, in the men's 500-meter speed skating. There was a tragic explanation—in 1961 a plane carrying many of our promising U.S. skaters and skiers and their coaches crashed in Brussels, killing them.

Now America was trying for a comeback, but the going was rough. The weather turned freaky—gale winds, heavy snows followed by quick thaws that turned bobsled and ski runs treacherous. U.S. skiers suffered two fractured legs, a sprained ankle, a dislocated shoulder, and a gashed head. A flu bug launched itself into team headquarters, felling some of the best girl speed skaters. The hope for a gold medal rested on the shoulders of slender, raven-haired, nineteen-year-old Peggy Fleming. She looked far too fragile to carry the load.

Peggy had done little skating before she was nine. Her father was an itinerant newspaper printer and the family—Mom, Dad, Peggy, and her three sisters—moved so often to wherever his business took him that there hadn't been an opportunity to take to the ice. She was an active child, however, and when they were living in Cleveland, her parents decided she should take lessons to work off some of her excess energy.

"Peggy didn't wobble at all," her sister Janice says. "She just started skating as though she knew what she was doing."

It was soon clear that she did, but her early training, unlike that of Golden Girls who had come before her, was pretty much catch-as-catch-can. She took lessons whenever she could, wherever the family happened to be living, until it became obvious that she indeed had a rare talent. The family decision was made: they would go where Peggy could have expert training. They chose Colorado Springs to be near the Broadmoor Hotel's ice school, where coach Carlo Fassi took Peggy in hand. The grueling training schedule that every champion goes through began. Practice, travel to meets, compete. Practice. Practice.

The trophies, medals, and titles began to pile up. At fifteen she won her first United States title, and she won that one four more times. She took the World Championship from 1966 through 1968.

After her 1968 win, President Lyndon B. Johnson honored her with a reception in the White House Rose

Garden, and Colorado Springs proclaimed "Peggy Fleming Day" and held a huge celebration with everybody from the governor down in attendance.

Her first taste of the Olympics was in 1964 at Innsbruck, the ancient and beautiful Tyrolean city. She came in sixth.

The chief stars of those Games were women. Blonde Russian Lydia Skoblikova, the speed-skating marvel who had won two golds at Squaw Valley, became the first person, man or woman, ever to win four Gold Medals in a single Olympics. She swept the speed events, taking the 500-, 1000-, 1500- and 5000-meter races. Two cheerful French sisters, Christine and Marielle Goitschel, divided the skiing gold medals between them, Christine taking the slalom and Marielle the giant slalom. A long way from the days women had to compete against men if they wanted to enter!

Four years after Innsbruck, Peggy waited in the wings for her turn to come at the 1968 Grenoble Olympics. She remembered early meets she had entered "just for fun." The first was a local affair and ten-year-old Peggy was both thrilled and surprised to come in first. This, she thought, was great: applause, attention, a nice prize, and all so easy! Why not keep it up? She entered a regional contest—and came in last! That was no fun. A sober Peggy sat down to think.

If I'm going to enter contests, she decided, I'd better be serious about it.

Her dad, who loved sports, helped her all he could. "It's not the hours of practice, Peggy," he coached. "It's the *quality* that counts."

Now, at the Olympics, as she skated onto the ice in the frothy chartreuse costume her mother had made, she had twenty thousand hours of quality practice behind her. It hadn't all been fun, as she'd once thought. There'd been disappointments, and sometimes she'd been lonely and felt left out of the things other girls did. Being a champion isn't all glamour.

She skated now to the haunting music of Tchaikovsky's *Pathétique,* and she seemed to float and whirl and soar with effortless ease. She was the only world-class skater who swung gently into turns, arching her body to pick up momentum instead of stroking powerfully with her legs. Reporters wrote about her "fragile grace" and "elegance." Some called her "the shy Bambi."

She knew that she was far ahead of other competitors in the school figures. She might have played it safe, giving a lovely but less demanding performance. But that was not for her. "I'm competing against myself," she said. "I'll skate as well as I can."

And she did. It was a 24-carat exhibition. She won her gold medal. Making her almost as happy was the fact that the three American girl speed skaters who'd been battling the flu bug—Mary Meyers, Dianne Holum, and Jennifer Fish—tied for the silver medal in the 500-meter race. Such a thing as a triple tie had never happened before in the Winter Olympics!

Peggy turned professional shortly after her Olympic win, and her career as an ice-show star has been as brilliant as it was when she was winning national, world, and Olympic titles.

"But it's different," she says. "There's more pressure in competition—knowing that thirty or more girls are out there wanting to beat you piles it on. In competition skating you skate to please the judges. In an ice show you want to please the people. You have to show them you're happy so they'll be happy, too."

And for a dozen years Peggy has been making audiences happy, first—and still—as a guest star of the fabulous Ice Follies, then in her TV specials that millions have watched, appearing in Holiday on Ice, touring in her own show, becoming the youngest skater ever inducted into the Skating Hall of Fame, serving as an Olympic TV commentator. And she coached the Colorado College Phi Delta Theta Red Barons in hockey.

"They weren't very good," she confesses. "But we all had fun."

In 1970, Peggy married Dr. Gregory Jenkins, a well-known California dermatologist, and they established their home in a San Francisco suburb. Seven years later she startled her fans by announcing that she was putting her career in deep freeze.

"But only temporarily," she grinned. "You see, Greg and I have started a family." Her grin widened.

"But after the baby's born, I'll be back to skating. It's a nice change from housework."

Andrew was born, and true to her promise it wasn't too long before Peggy was back with her beloved Ice Follies, in front of the cheering audiences who love her. She's limiting her performances to about eleven weeks a year now so that she can spend more time at home with her husband and little son.

"Maybe some television, too," she says with that elfin smile. "And perhaps movies. I intend to keep going as long as they want me."

And that will be a long, long time!

In the 1972 Winter Games a pretty Austrian girl, Beatrix Schuba, captured the figure-skating gold medal that Tenley and Carol and Peggy had won for the United States. Then came the Games of 1976. And Dorothy Hamill.

The girl with the glasses. Big, wonderful, oversized glasses worn not for style, but because she needs them to see. And if you think her eyesight hampers her, watch her go into a "Hamill camel," the famous move named after her: a camel spin, into a sit-spin with a spin coming out. It takes your breath away.

Dorothy is something of the homey type. She loves to spend time around her house, likes to cook and bake (and is good at it), is a great reader. She collects turtles and jewelry. She likes gothic novels and soap operas. Sweets are a weakness of hers, but she knows when she has to cut down and "do the cottage cheese bit." She likes to dawdle through a foamy bath or do her fingernails. She loves music.

That shows in her marvelous skating. She's been described as "music on ice"—all rhythm and tempo. The tempo is apt to be fiery. Dorothy moves on ice with a liquid speed that makes many other skaters appear to be in slow motion.

She was born in the small Connecticut town of Riverside, where her father, Chalmers Hamill, a prominent business executive, and her mother, Carol, had established their comfortable family home. There was plenty of space to romp and play, and older brother Sandy and younger sister Marcia to have fun with. Later when the championship route began to keep Dorothy away from home (once she didn't see her brother and sister for almost a whole year), she missed them badly.

The local pond was her first rink; her first skates a nifty pair of $5.95 strap-ons. But very soon the talent showed and the familiar routine began. Eleven years of it, much of that time spent in seven-hours-a-day, six-times-a-week, eleven-months-of-the-year practice.

Sonja Henie had her idol, the dancer Pavlova; and Dorothy soon had hers: Mikhail Baryshnikov, the famous Russian ballet artist, now a leading dancer in the United States. Like him, she loves to interpret the music with feeling, and like him she never shows the muscle-tensing preparation for a leap lesser artists seem unable to conceal. She seems to drift up and hang in mid-air before completing an unbelievable one-and-a-half revolutions, then, perhaps, going into a dizzying spin.

One roadblock almost kept her from the goal she wanted: Dorothy was overwhelmingly shy. When she was in third grade she didn't want to be in the Thanksgiving Day play with all the other children. The thought of the audience made her weep with nervousness. That nervousness before a performance has never quite left her. It was—and is—something she couldn't shake off. But she could learn to handle it through dedication and willpower. And she did.

Sometimes her hard-earned poise deserts her. In a world meet in Munich the crowd booed as Dorothy skated into the spotlight. For a moment she stood pinned like a butterfly in the light, then she fled, weeping, to the side of the rink and her father's arms. Only when she was made to understand that the crowd was booing the low scores the judges had given the previous skater, not her, could she return to the rink. At a United States meet she saw a sign that read, "Dorothy, Wicked Witch of the West." She couldn't go on until she learned that her own fans were holding the sign, and it was meant to warn her competition.

Like more than one famous actor and actress, she suffers from this preshow stage fright. But once she's performing, that fright leaves her—as it does them. Out on the rink, the ice beneath her silvery skates, the huge lights beaming down on her, everything else slides away. "I feel good," she says. "I feel alive. I'm happy."

But though she's often plagued by anxiety, and close friends call her a mass of emotions, Dorothy can be wackily funny, too, doing takeoffs and imitations that make people howl. Once while the United States figure-skating team was waiting to do a television interview, Dorothy pre-empted an executive's huge mahogany desk, grabbed a fat cigar, stuck it in her mouth, and began dictating zany messages to her fellow skaters. There is no telling what Dorothy will do.

Except win titles: the United States Championship three times, the World Championship, the Olympics . . .

Dorothy, like other lovely skating stars, turned pro after winning the Olympics. She made her first TV special for ABC. ("I chose them because they were so nice to me at the Olympics.") It was filmed in Canada with an enchanting group of Canadian children. The month was February. The temperature was 20 degrees below zero. Dorothy had the flu and a temperature of 102. None of that showed. The show was pure joy, highlighted by her whirlwind delicate performance and her luminous smile.

Later Dorothy signed with the Ice Capades and embarked on her new career with the same charm, skill, and shyness she had as an amateur. Onstage that shyness vanishes.

And offstage there's one thing she always tries to

do: give autographs. "When I was real little," she says, "I tried to get a celebrity's autograph, and failed. I was miserably disappointed." She doesn't want any other little girl, future champion or not, to suffer in that way.

# VIII

Women's speed skating wasn't added to the Olympics until 1932, and the United States women have only managed to capture a few gold medals since then. And until Eric Heiden's five-medal triumph at Lake Placid in 1980, the men hadn't done any better. There are only about a hundred speed skaters in the United States, as against 300,000 training and competing in the USSR, which can be consistently counted on to be among the winners. One reason for our scant number and lack of medalists is the dearth of training facilities. The *only* 400-meter track in the whole country is in a little town named West Allis, Wisconsin, while in the

Soviet Union tracks abound. It's pretty difficult to train for speed and distance without proper facilities!

Yet of all the winter events at Innsbruck in 1976—Alpine and Nordic skiing, ski jump, ice hockey, tobogganing—it was the women skaters who brought home the gold: Dorothy Hamill for figure skating, and Sheila Young, the whiz-kid of speed.

Sheila's a cute 130-pound, five-foot-four-inch, brown-haired, breezy type of girl who chatters unflappably with reporters, and looks as docile as a pet pussycat until she blasts away from the starting line and zooms down her lane. Then she's all cougar.

She comes from a sports-oriented family. Her father and mother were both champion cycle racers and top-notch skaters. Older sister Susan was a champion speed skater, brothers Jamie and Roger both excellent athletes (Roger won the cycling gold medal in both the National and Pan American Games).

Sheila is a champion cyclist as well as speed skater. She is the only one, male or female, ever to be a world champion in two completely different sports in the same year: speed skating and cycle racing in 1973.

"I could ride a two-wheeler—without training wheels—when I was four," she says. "I didn't get around to speed skating until I was nine."

Shelia was born in Birmingham, Michigan, where there was plenty of opportunity for winter sports. Her mother died when she was thirteen, and shortly after that the family moved to Detroit. They were a close-knit group, sharing household chores (her dad did the cooking, and even baked bread). Money wasn't too plentiful, so most of their entertainment came from outdoor sports, whose costs were minimal.

"I couldn't afford a baby sitter," Mr. Young says, "so when I went speed skating, the kids came along."

"I wasn't that interested in skating when I was little," Sheila says. "The family would take off, I didn't want to go. When I was eight, my mother said I could have a portable TV if I'd join the rest of them. I said no."

But maybe it was the TV that kept her mind on skating. The next year she decided she wanted to try and she asked for her portable.

Her mother shook her head. "That was for last year," she said. Sheila decided to skate anyway and, once she had started, it was speed that fascinated her. Soon she was entering local races—and winning them.

She trained on a nearby lake Tuesday and Thursday evenings and Wednesdays after school. Weekends were for races. She began winning junior championships.

"I didn't really have any bigger goals," she says, "until I met Peter Schotting."

Peter, a red-haired, stubborn Dutchman and top skating coach, took one look at Sheila's style and stamina and said, "Train with me for a year and you'll be a world champion."

That piqued Sheila's competitive spirit, of which

she has an abundance. She also has the dedication every champion must have. She began training in earnest—and the training for speed skating is as grueling as any you can imagine. She skated four hours a day. She did long-distance running and sprints and dryland exercises (in one of them she imitates a Groucho. Marx walk, her upper body parallel to the ground, her legs bent at the knees). She took up cycling originally to help improve her skating—cycling could be done during the summer. You can't stop skating for three months and win top competition. Sheila didn't know that she would soon be competing for national and world titles in two separate sports.

"That really drains you," she says. "Keeping up the pace not only physically but mentally in two sports is tough."

That didn't stop Sheila Young. A little over a year after she began training with Schotting, she won the World Sprint Championship. In 1972 she missed getting the Olympic bronze in speed skating by 8/100 of a second—the blink of an eye! Undaunted, she went on to win the World Championship in 1973, and that same year set a world record for 500 meters. She captured the title again in 1975. And she won the Nationals in cycle racing in both 1971 and 1973.

She got her most dramatic world cyclist title at San Sebastian, Spain. No one expected her to take the title—after all, Galina Ermolaeva of the USSR was competing, and Galina had won that title six times in a row. Galina was in prime condition and had been

84

training at the finest of the Soviets' very superior centers. Sheila made her successful way up through the qualifying rounds. Then came the semifinals. Sheila set her feet hard on the pedals. She pumped around the track with demon ferocity. She won over Galina. But would she—could she—take the championship?

There were three races to decide the finalists. Sheila was in the first, pedaling as she never had pedaled before. Racing bikes have no gears and no brakes. You get on and go for dear life, and that's it.

She was slashing down the course when Eva Zajickova of Czechoslovakia, maybe through one of those errors that can happen, maybe through sheer determination to win, cut in ahead of her. There was a horrendous crash. Sheila was cut and bleeding on her arms and legs, an ugly gash in her head. United States officials requested the disqualification of the Czech girl. The officials refused.

"The race will be run over," they said.

How could Sheila possibly contend? "Paste me together!" she demanded. The doctors did—bandaging her wounds, stapling her cut scalp together. Sheila got on her bike, pain, wounds, and all. She won that race—and the next one—to take first place.

"You must be the toughest girl in the world," one reporter said in awe.

"Nope," Sheila said. "Just the most determined."

Now she had other things to think about: skating and the Winter Olympics.

"Doesn't it bother you that your sports are considered secondary in the United States?" an American reporter asked her.

Sheila thought that over, and then nodded. "Yes, it does, sort of," she conceded. "But I'm proud of my sports. I get a lot of recognition in other countries. I wish my sports were bigger here, but not for the glory. I wish they were recognized more because people are missing a chance to see how exciting they are." She thought a minute more and then added, "My sports have been terrific to me. I've gone all over the world—places I'd never have got to except for competing. I've made good friends, and traveling and meeting people helped me develop my personality. When I was a kid I was sort of introverted. I'm not any more. Sure, I've paid the price—you have to do that to get to the top. But it was worth it. I wouldn't trade places with anybody."

She was training hard. Her goal, she said, was to capture one medal at the Olympics. And she'd met a man she knew she clicked with. His name was Jim Ochowicz; his home, Milwaukee. Jim and her brother Roger were friends, both of them cyclists. Jim asked her brother to set him up with a date—and Sheila filled in. Later, when she was training at the United States long-distance rink in West Allis, she lived with the Ochowiczes, not far from the rink. She was like a family member; Jim was like a brother.

"It was kind of funny," she says, "when we realized the way we liked each other was something else again."

Realize it they did, more and more. "But we didn't want to get married until after I'd been to the Olympics," she says. "I wanted that medal. We didn't want kids yet—marriage right away wasn't important to us."

So they moved in together. It wasn't the greatest of all apartments. The bedroom was small, and the closet housed their two racing bikes. Neither one of them had too many clothes, and their racing bikes couldn't be tethered outdoors; they cost a lot of money and someone might steal them. Neither Jim nor Sheila was what you might call a meticulous housekeeper (there were apt to be sweat socks on the kitchen table and skates in the living room). They also discovered that neither of them was a very good cook, which made meal-getting a bit of a problem. But they managed.

And then came the 1976 Innsbruck Winter Olympics, and the chance for that speed-skating medal Sheila wanted. Jim (she calls him Oach) was there, though they'd had to sell Sheila's racing bike to help pay his way over. Sheila smuggled him into the girls' dorm one day so he could see where she was staying and maybe put a good-luck seal on it.

Her coach, her father, and her stepmother (Mr. Young had remarried a few years earlier) were there. They were all rooting for Sheila. There was enormous pressure on her because she was one of the few people on the United States team, male or female, who anybody believed *might* capture a gold medal.

The race for the 500- began. Coach Schotting had bought the American team electric-blue nylon suits that fit so tight the girls looked as though they'd been poured into them. In that streamlined outfit, her dad called her "Moon Girl" and the spectators named her "the American Frogman." Sockless Sheila knew it felt right.

"I never wear socks," she explains. "With my bare toes I have a better rapport with my skates. I can really *feel* them."

She certainly must have been feeling them that day. She slashed her way to a gold medal in the 500-, took a silver in the 1500-, and got a third-place bronze in the 1000- —making her the *first* American athlete, male or female, to win three medals in one Winter Olympics.

After her third win, President Ford called to congratulate her. Sheila wasn't there. She was out seeing the town and reveling in the victory with Oach, who was so proud of her he was about to burst.

Sheila went on to take the World Championship in Norway. Then it was back to the pad to help Oach get ready for the Olympic cyclist championship.

"I wish they had an Olympic cyclist championship I could enter," Sheila said wistfully. "But Women's Lib hasn't caught up with that yet."

Sheila announced her decision to retire from amateur sports competition after her World and Olympic championships. There weren't any glamour jobs ahead, as there are for figure skaters. She'd known that all along.

"That doesn't really matter," she says—and adds with a big grin, "not that I'd have turned the money down. We could use it."

And she and Oach could. They're happily married now and have their plans for a sports-oriented business, maybe coaching—certainly something to do with the things they love best.

"We've done what we wanted to," Sheila says, pushing her dark hair from her forehead. And then that marvelous grin splits her face. "Now we're going to raise a whole batch of little speed skaters and cyclists. And maybe," she adds, "by the time they come along, our country will have some top-notch facilities where they can train."

IX

Outstanding as Sheila Young's three-medal performance was at Innsbruck, a Soviet woman, Tatiana
Averina, collected the most medals: gold in the 100-
and 5000-meter races, bronze in the 500- and 1500-.
Tatiana hadn't been handicapped, as Sheila was, by a
lack of training facilities. She trained at the Medeo
Sports Center which, as one reporter put it, looks like
the Taj Mahal compared to anything in America. The
ice there is the best in the world, and is frozen nine
months out of the year.

Medeo is just one example of the advantages for
training that the Soviets (and most Iron Curtain coun-

tries) enjoy. Throughout the country there are free sports clubs in practically every village, town, and city where all manner of athletic training can be had. Children as young as six begin participating: 1,800,000 Soviet children attend under the tutelage of some forty-seven thousand coaches. Those who show real promise in any given sport have a chance to attend one of the country's thirty-two special sports boarding schools. Such assistance to budding talented athletes obviously pays off: since joining the Olympics in 1952, the USSR has won more medals than any other country.

At the 1952 Games in Helsinki a girl named Galina Zybina captured one of those medals—a gold one. The odds against her ever reaching the Olympics had been enormous.

Galina's childhood home was a small isolated house near the Neva River. In the bitter winter of 1942, she and her mother and small brother were huddled in that house, trying to stave off cold and hunger.

Hitler's Nazi armies had invaded Russia during the past summer. Minsk had fallen, Kiev and Orel. Moscow was endangered. The siege of Leningrad raged. Every man capable of bearing arms—and many women—were fighting valiantly. Galina's father was at the front.

The task of survival for the rest of the little family had fallen on Galina's thin shoulders. Snow piled high outside the door. The wind was freezing cold. The food they had eked out so carefully for weeks as they hoped for some rescue party to bring supplies was nearly gone. The small fire on the hearth could not warm the cold room.

On the bed in the corner her small brother and mother lay grievously ill. Trying to hide her worry, Galina smoothed the quilts over them.

"I must go for water," she whispered. Her mother tried to smile encouragement—such a ghost of a smile that Galina turned quickly to hide her tears.

Pulling on her coat, she braved the frigid outdoors, carrying the tin pail. Battling the wind, she forced herself to the edge of the river. Every hour she had to make this trip, breaking the new ice over the hole she had made in it. Otherwise, it would freeze so solidly she would not be able to fill the bucket.

She was very weak. It was hard to carry the water. Once back home she set it near the fire and then struggled out again, searching through the scrub trees until she managed to gather a small armful of dead branches. Exhausted, she made her way back to the house.

She built up the fire as much as she dared. Wood was so hard to find! She did not know how many more times she could make the trip. With no heat they would freeze.

There was no more thin potato soup left. They had eaten that yesterday, one small bowlful each. Now there was only part of a loaf of black bread and some tea.

"If only someone would come through and help us," she thought desperately. Then she thought of her father, fighting at the front, and tried to be brave.

She cut two slivers of bread, made a pot of tea, fed her mother and brother.

"I've already had mine," she lied, trying not to show how hungry she was. Her mother's lips moved, but the words were too faint to hear. Gently Galina eased her mother down onto the pillow.

That night her mother died. Now there was just her small brother and herself. All the next day she tried to minister to him, feeding him the last bit of bread, helping him sip the tea, leaving him only to keep the river water hole open. But the cold and the hunger had taken too much of his strength. He died before daybreak.

Galina was alone. The house creaked with cold. Every hour seemed endless, the trip to the water hole longer and harder, until at last she could go no more. She used the last of the tea and then for two days she had only water. After that she doesn't remember.

When the men with supplies broke through to the house they found Galina so near death that they were afraid she would die before they could get her to a hospital, but some spark of the will to live kept her alive. Slowly but surely she began to mend. When she was strong enough they gave her the last bit of heartbreaking news: her father had been killed at the front.

Galina was sent to a Home for Orphans, a pleasant, cheerful place with the best of care, but the ordeal she'd been through had taken its toll. She was frail and thin, lost in her utter loneliness. For many weeks she took little interest in the games the other children played.

Gradually she began to get better. From time to time she joined the other children at play. They welcomed her easily enough but, as children will, they teased her for being so skinny. They called her "tadpole." And that made her want to fight back. Stubbornly she set about exercising, building herself back up, regaining her strength. And she set a secret goal for herself: she would become good enough at sports to enter competition!

The two sports she liked best were the javelin and the shotput. Stubbornly she trained. And improved. There was no teasing now. Galina Zybina was accepted into the Leningrad Juvenile Sports School. That was an honor.

She trained under coach Victor Alexeyev—and she trained harder than anyone else. "Because I have farther to go," she said. When she entered the Leningrad High School of Mechanics (she was interested in the science of optics), she continued her work with Alexeyev after school. And in 1949 she set records in both of her chosen sports. Her first international victory came at the Bucharest Stadium in Romania. And now Galina's heart and efforts were set on the 1952 Olympics.

Helsinki hosted the Games that year, with the

president of Finland formally proclaiming the XV Games open at the close of the parade of nations and colorful ceremonies. Galina, in her smart white flannel uniform and red tie, was in that parade.

She was entered in two events: the shotput and javelin. The javelin was scheduled first. To her bitter disappointment she came in fourth. Though most people would think that being fourth in the world was no bad showing, Galina felt herself a complete failure. She had tried so hard! She had wanted so much to be the very best.

"Not even the bronze!" she wept. "I shouldn't be here! I've let everyone down!"

"Tomorrow is another day," her coach told her. "You'll do better—you'll see. Come along now. We will see Helsinki!"

He took her on a tour of the city, pointing out the sights, stopping to look in shop windows, telling little jokes that coaxed her to smile. Taking her mind off her disappointment. Little by little he pushed away her sense of failure.

"You see," he told her. "Looking back is no good. It makes you gloomy. Look ahead, Galina. That is the best way."

Galina went to bed that night full of hope and resolution. When the shotput was called the next day she was ready. Cheeks glowing, blonde hair tied back with bright red ribbons, she looked full of confidence.

She stepped into the ring, weighed the shotput in her hand for a moment, whirled, gave a powerful throw—the best of any of the contestants. On her second throw she did even better: she made a new world's record.

And so the little girl whom the odds would have counted out reached the goal she had set her heart on—and worked so hard for. Galina Zybina had won her gold medal.

There was another girl whom the odds would most surely have counted out, without hesitation. Her name was Wilma Rudolph. It's a name to remember.

Wilma was born June 23, 1940, in the small town of St. Bethlehem, Tennessee, the twentieth of twenty-two children. Her father was a porter; her mother did housework for various families in the community.

Soon after her birth the family moved to Clarksville. It was there that Wilma, at age four, was stricken with pneumonia and scarlet fever. She was a desperately sick little girl, and the illness left her with a crippled left leg.

She couldn't walk. When she tried, her leg buckled and she fell. Doctors in the small town gave no hope for her recovery. But Mrs. Rudolph was not going to settle for that. Bundling Wilma into a blanket, she took her by bus to Nashville, where there were specialists. Wilma was examined and tested. The doctors' verdict was not encouraging. She would have to have special treatments, and even with them the doctors would guarantee nothing.

"We've got hope," Mrs. Rudolph said. "That's good enough to go on."

"You'll have to bring her to the hospital for daily massage," the doctors said.

It was over forty miles from the family home to Nashville. There was no way Mrs. Rudolph could take time from her work to make that trip daily—or afford the fare.

"Teach me to do the massage," she said. And they did.

Every day when her work was finished and the evening meal for the big family cooked and eaten, Mrs. Rudolph massaged Wilma's leg. Once a week on her day off she took Wilma to the hospital for treatment. She taught the older children how to do the massage so they could help. It cut into their playtime and they grumbled a little.

"Wilma has to have her chance," their mother said firmly. "We're all one family. We share the good and the bad."

At the end of two years the doctors saw only the smallest improvement and they told Mrs. Rudolph as kindly as they could that she should accept Wilma's crippled leg.

"I've got faith," Mrs. Rudolph said with dignity. "My baby will walk."

She kept up the treatments. Wilma began to manage a kind of hopping walk. When she was six, the doctors made a brace for her leg and she could get along better. Then they substituted a clumsy high-topped shoe, and Wilma, cheerful as a chipmunk, clomped about happily.

One of her brothers had put up a basketball hoop in the backyard and, choosing sides, the kids played endless games. Wilma refused to be left out.

"But when she's on our side, we lose," a brother complained.

"Winning isn't the only thing in life," Mrs. Rudolph told him. "Mind you count Wilma in—and mind you take your turn at the massaging."

At school children teased Wilma about her clumsy shoe. "How long you gonna wear that thing?" a little boy taunted.

"When I can walk, I'll *show* you!" Wilma retorted.

And the leg was improving. It felt different to Wilma—as though it was alive, or something. One day when her mother came home from work she stopped in her tracks, staring. There was Wilma, both shoes off, running about the yard, dribbling the basketball and shooting baskets.

Afraid Wilma might have damaged her leg, Mrs. Rudolph rushed her to the doctor in spite of her protests that she felt just fine. The doctors examined Wilma and agreed with her: she no longer needed the ugly shoe!

There was jubilation in the family that night, and the next day Wilma's father brought her a present. She opened it eagerly. It was a pair of shiny, patent leather shoes—the first she had ever owned. She put them on joyfully and danced about the house, singing with happiness.

"They're for Sundays," her father warned. "They're going-to-church shoes."

Wilma put her beautiful new shoes away carefully, and she wore them proudly every Sunday. And every chance she could get, she was in the yard barefoot, playing basketball. "Making up for lost time," her mother said fondly.

When she entered Clarksville High School at thirteen, Wilma tried out for basketball and made the team. She also won the nickname "Skeeter." "Always buzzing around," the coach said. "Like a mosquito."

By the time she was fifteen, she'd grown to her full five-foot-eleven, a graceful, willowy, beautiful girl and an all-state basketball player. She was also a track star.

That year Ed Temple, the women's track coach

at Tennessee A and I State University, saw her run in a track meet. He was building up his team of Tiger-belles, wanting to bring more recognition to the black university, and he knew that Wilma would be an asset.

"Go to college?" Wilma gasped. It was beyond her wildest dreams. With twenty-two children there was simply no money for any such thing. "How much will it cost?"

"Nothing. You'll have a scholarship. I think you can be a champion—if you want to."

Want to! College and becoming a champion! It was almost too much to take in.

"Oh, my!" her mother breathed. "None of the others ever had anything like this come along."

Her father was dubious. "She ain't never been away from home," he worried. "She's been protected like. She don't know about things."

"How am I going to find out, if I don't try?" Wilma pleaded.

"You had bad times as a child. I don't want no more of them for you."

"It's a mighty big chance for her," Mrs. Rudolph said softly.

Her father was silent for a long time, closed in with his own thoughts. Wilma watched anxiously, her eyes bright with hope, hardly daring to breathe. At last her father raised his head and looked at her.

"You want to go, child?" Wilma nodded, not daring to speak. And after another long moment of silence her father agreed. "Then it's settled," he said.

She was soon to discover that training under Coach Temple was tougher than almost anything she had ever imagined. There was none of the easygoing home life she was so fond of. Temple was exacting. Training periods were tough—and started early in the morning. Wilma loved to sleep. Some days she just didn't get going. She was thirty minutes late one morning.

"One lap around the track for each late minute," the coach ordered. Wilma did thirty laps. The next morning she showed up early.

She practiced starts until her takeoff was jet-stream. She ran distance races. Exercised. She began to win races—nine of them in one day at a Philadelphia meet.

And she was homesick. "I want to go home," she told her coach.

He gave her a long look. "All right. Don't come back unless you mean it."

Wilma went home. It was wonderful to be back with the big, loving family, to eat her mama's good cooking, not to have to get up on the dot if she didn't want to. But as the days passed, she grew quieter and quieter.

"What is it, child?" her mother asked.

Wilma bit her lip and looked down.

"You're thinking about what you're missing out on."

Wilma nodded.

Her mother was silent a long time. "You can go back if you want to," she said then. "But you have to be sure this time. It's not fair to you or the people at the college to keep changing your mind. You think on it, Wilma."

Wilma did. A few days later she was back on campus and back in training.

She was only sixteen when she went to the Melbourne Olympics in 1956. They were held in the unusual months of late November and early December that year—the first time the Games had ever been held in the Southern Hemisphere, where those are summer months. She was still in the learning stage and she didn't do well in her individual events, but she helped the United States relay team come in third, and won a bronze medal. No one would ever have guessed that she had once been crippled.

She was fired with determination to go to the next Olympics—and to win. She trained as she never had before. Her improvement was remarkable. She had style, speed—everything going for her. But she had fallen in love with a boy named Robert Eldridge. And a baby was coming.

It was Coach Temple who helped her tell her folks. "I want her to come back to college after the baby's born," he finished.

Her father was crushed, and he turned away from what the coach was saying. "She's going to take care of her child, like her mama," he said with finality. "That's her place now."

Robert wanted her to marry him and it was a hard, hard time for Wilma. So many things to try to think through; so very difficult to find the right answers.

"If we get married," she said to Robert slowly, "we'll never finish college. There'll be a living to make before we're ready ... home to take care of, more babies to tend. . . . All the rest will end." He started to speak, to try to persuade her, but she stopped him. She faced him squarely. "I can't marry you now," she said. "It's not the right thing."

She held firm to that decision. She'd made one mistake, and she knew it. Not going back to school, not using the talent she'd been given, would compound it. And so she stayed home that year. Her baby was born, and she was a darling—happy, healthy— she won everyone over to her. Especially Wilma's father, who now smiled again.

Leaving the baby in her mother's care, Wilma returned to Tennessee U. She worked as she never had worked before—"making up for lost time," as her mother had once said. She became the Tigerbelles' star runner, and they had plenty of good ones—the fastest in the country. She had two years to get ready for the 1960 Rome Olympics—two years crammed with training, tours, meets, trophy winning, record breaking, studying for her BA in education with a minor in psychology—and more training.

Wilma Rudolph managed it all, and when the United States team flew off to Rome, she rated tops in America's hopes for the coveted gold. It was blazing hot in Rome. The U.S. contenders suffered many setbacks. On Thursday—which became known as Black Thursday in the American camp—many favored Americans failed.

Then it was Friday. Wilma's first event, the 100-meter dash, was called. She dug in at the starting blocks. The gun barked. Maria Itkina of the USSR was away first. She held the lead for 25 meters. Then Wilma, moving with the combined speed and grace only she possessed, forged ahead. At 50 meters she was way out in front. At 75 she lengthened the lead. She breezed in to an easy win. *One gold medal in her possession!*

Monday she repeated her performance in the 200 meters, coming in an astonishing four yards ahead of the second-place winner. *Another gold medal!*

Thursday was the relay race with four Tiger-belles, with Wilma as the anchor woman, making up the team. The first three girls ran beautifully. The team was two yards out in front when the baton was passed to Wilma.

And something went wrong! The runner fumbled the baton in her pass to Wilma!

The crowd gasped. Wilma had to stop dead to get the baton. Jutta Heine, anchor woman for the German team, raced into the lead. Wilma set after her. Her long, fluid strides seemed to burn up the track.

She was running at a speed no one could believe. She pulled up even with the German girl. They fought it out, stride for stride. The crowd was on its feet screaming with excitement. In the last split second, Wilma thrust ahead. The United States team had won! *Wilma had her third gold medal.* It was the first time in the history of the Games that an American woman had won three gold medals for running.

They called her the Black Gazelle. They called her incomparable. The famous Jesse Owens, himself a four-time Olympic track gold medalist, said she was the most beautiful thing that ever ran. And she was as gracious as she was graceful. Never too tired to grant an interview, pose for a news photographer, or sign an autograph—and thousands of people wanted it. Never complaining—not even when fans pulled the shoes from her feet for souvenirs. She just kept on going in her stocking feet.

Following the Rome Olympics, Coach Temple took his team on a triumphant tour of Europe. They competed in rain, heat, and cold, sometimes after only four hours of sleep. They competed in Athens, Amsterdam, Cologne, Wuppertal, Frankfurt, Berlin, and London. And they always won.

Back home there were cheering crowds and celebrations, interviews and honors. President Kennedy invited Wilma to the White House. European sportswriters named her Sportsman of the Year, the first American woman ever so honored. In the United

States Wilma was voted Woman Athlete of the Year.

"Will you be going back in 1964?" a reporter asked her.

"Only as a spectator," she answered with a smile. "I have some things to do."

Since that day Wilma has found a great many things to do, and marriage to Robert came first. She got her degree from Tennessee U. She wrote her autobiography, which became a bestseller and was made into a prime-time movie on NBC television. She served as Goodwill Ambassador for the United States to French West Africa and as a member of the U.S. Olympic Committee, acted as a special consultant to the Tennessee Department of Economic and Community Development. She was inducted into the Black Athletes Hall of Fame, one of only three women then included. She was the first woman selected as a director for the Annual Muhammad Ali Track Meet. She taught at UCLA. It would be hard to list all of the things Wilma has done.

And *is* doing, for Wilma is not about to retire. She lectures throughout the country and is today one of the ten most popular speakers at colleges in America. She's involved with youth programs, appears as a guest on TV talk shows. She is an NBC radio commentator for *Olympic Odyssey*. She is currently working on her master's degree at Peabody College in Nashville.

Wilma and Robert make their home in Hendersonville, Tennessee. They have four great children:

Yolanda, Djuana, Xurry, and Robert, Jr. All the children are good at sports, and both Yolanda and Djuana are track stars.

"We're going to make it to the Olympics!" Djuana says happily.

And with Wilma Rudolph for their mother, no one would be the least bit surprised.

Wyomia Tyus proudly beams over her four Olympic medals, three gold and one silver, which she earned in running events at Tokyo in 1964 and Mexico City in 1968. She set a new world's record in the 100-meter race in 1968.

Willye White leaping to victory in the broad jump at a U.S.-Poland meet in 1963. Five times Willye was on the U.S. Olympic track and field team.

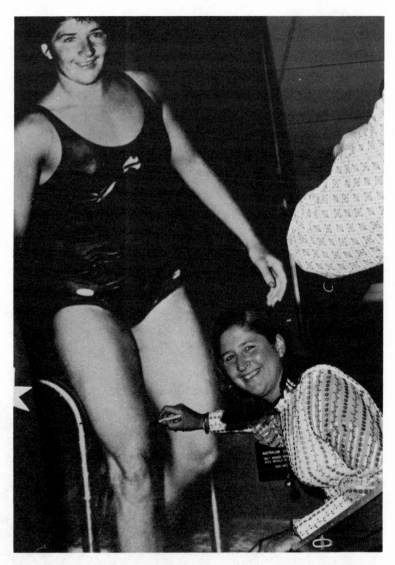

At the Swimming Hall of Fame in Florida, Australian Dawn Fraser signs a photo of herself, taken in Olympic days. She placed first in swimming three times: in 1956, 1960, and in 1964, at the age of twenty-seven.

The "Marvelous Mama of Holland," Fanny Blankers-Koen, leaps over the hurdles at the London Games of 1948, at the age of thirty. She captured four gold medals: for the hurdles, and for the 100-meter, 200-meter, and relay races.

Olga Korbut of the U.S.S.R. grins over her three gold-medal victory in gymnastics at the Munich Games in 1972.

Olga in flight.

Romanian Nadia Comaneci, age fourteen, on the balance beam at Montreal in 1976, where she dazzled the world and won three gold medals.

Nadia demonstrates the breath-taking form that won her, time and again, the unprecedented perfect score of 10.0.

Cathy Rigby, twice a member of the U.S. Olympic gymnastic team and several-time World Cup Champion, works out on the balance beam.

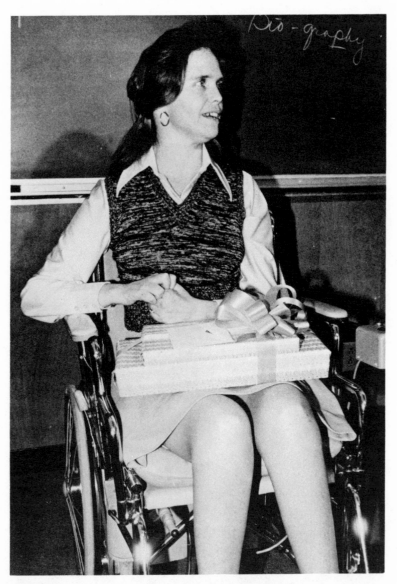

Jill Kinmont, an Olympic hopeful for 1956, was permanently disabled in an accident at a skiing competition in 1955. After years of therapy and training, Jill became a teacher of children with reading disabilities. She is pictured in her classroom.

XI

One of the track stars Wilma Rudolph helped train at the summer clinics run by coach Ed Temple was a little sixteen-year-old named Wyomia Tyus.

Wyomia was born in Griffin, Georgia, and home was a dairy farm just outside the town. She was the youngest child and the only girl, and it didn't take her long to learn that it was no bad deal to have three big brothers who thought she was just about the cutest thing that ever came down the pike. Of course they took turns bossing her, too, but that in its way was sort of nice—it showed they cared about her.

Life on the farm was fun, with plenty of freedom

to run and play, and all kinds of outdoor magic to discover: the places where field flowers bloomed, the song a stream sang, how sweet the hay smelled in the summer sun—wonderful things a city child misses. There was work, too—plenty of it! Running a dairy farm adds up to endless chores, from sterilizing milk pails to cleaning the barn. The Tyus family raised most of their own food, too, so there were rows on rows of vegetables to tend—and at harvest time the canning to do. But it was a good life, and Wyomia loved it.

When she was six she entered first grade in Griffin. She was a good little student, but what she liked best was dancing in the May Day Festival every year, and the track and field activities. It was wonderful to line up for the races and speed away down the track, beating her playmates most of the time.

"She sure can run!" one of her brothers said proudly. "You gimme that blue ribbon. I'll take care of it for you."

When Wyomia was fourteen, disaster struck the Tyus family. Their home burned to the ground. They fought the fire fiercely, doing everything they could to save the house, but there were no fire trucks to race to their rescue, and the battle was too unequal. They were left homeless. There wasn't enough money to rebuild. They were forced to move to Griffin, where her father could get work. Just a year later he died suddenly and Mrs. Tyus was left with four children to bring up. She found work in a laundry and the boys helped, taking odd jobs where they could find them. Wyomia took on most of the cooking and the household chores. They worked together and kept the home going.

When Wyomia was ready for high school she enrolled at Fairmont. Now she was into everything! She joined the choir and sang in the concerts and recitals they gave. She was a member of 4H, the farm-oriented national club for young people. If she wasn't singing or at one of her club meetings, she was on the basketball court practicing with her team or out on the track.

"What you want to be doing boys' things all the time for?" one brother demanded. "Dancing, now that's all right for a girl, and singing. You ought to let running be."

Neither her mother nor her brothers were enthusiastic about her sports activities. They weren't, they felt, proper girl-type things.

"You're getting to be a young lady now," Mama said gently. "Maybe you should listen some to your brothers. They mean you well."

Wyomia knew that, but she loved track and basketball, knew she was good at both, and didn't think either made her a bit unladylike. She overrode their disapproval.

She attended her first big track meet when she was in tenth grade. Just as he had spotted Wilma Rudolph a few years earlier, Coach Temple spotted Wyomia now. He liked what he saw.

"Want to come to the high-school girls' Track and Field Clinic in Nashville this summer?" he asked.

Did she! Of course! But could she? There were three big brothers and her mother to convince. It took a bit of doing. Maybe knowing that Ed Temple picked only the best for his clinics helped. It was a proud thing to have one's sister chosen as among the best in the nation.

The 1961 clinic was the first of three Wyomia was to attend. She found them inspiring, as tough as she'd heard they would be, and terrific training grounds. It was a thrill to have Wilma Rudolph as one of her coaches. During those three summers Wyomia went annually to the National AAU Women and Girls' Track and Field Championship meets. In her second summer she established her first American records for her age group in the 50- and 75-yard dashes and made the United States Women's Track and Field Team for the first time. In their overseas tour through Germany, Poland, Russia, and England she did herself (and the team) proud. Wyomia Tyus was on her way to Olympic gold.

She entered Tennessee State U on a scholarship after graduating from high school. Now she was one of the famed Tigerbelles, as Wilma had been. And in 1964, when the Americans headed for Tokyo and the XVIII Olympiad, Wyomia Tyus was with them.

Tokyo had waited twenty-four years for the Olympics. It had been scheduled to play host in

1940, but World War II was raging and no Games were held. In ancient Greece, wars stopped for the Olympics—all hostilities were suspended and friend and foe alike attended the renowned Games. Alas, in modern times the opposite is true. So Tokyo had to wait until the Olympic Committee scheduled Games there.

Now everything was in splendid readiness. At exactly 1:00 P.M. on opening day there was a burst of music from the north chute of the giant stadium and a brilliantly uniformed band swung onto the brick-red track. The opening ceremonies had begun. Wyomia Tyus, in the American team's powder-blue uniform and cowboy hat, marched proudly with the United States delegation.

Wyomia won her first Olympic gold medal in Tokyo, for the 100-meter dash. She won her second in 1968 in Mexico City, and captured another one in the 400-meter relay. And in the years between she held five world records, was National AAU champion in the 100- four times, and International champion in the Pan American Games. She is the only woman ever to win the 100-meters in two consecutive Olympics. And on top of all that, she served as the United States Goodwill Ambassador to Africa—an honor Jesse Owens, the famed black runner and everybody's hero, had held before her.

Wyomia retired in 1968 and moved to Los Angeles, where she married Art Simburg, and where their daughter, Simone, was born. She taught physical education in junior and senior high school, and after five years returned to the track as a professional, joining the newly created International Track Association. As of this writing she has been undefeated on the circuit. The list of activities she manages to cram into her schedule is impressive: on the Advisory Board of the Women's Sports Foundation, the Post Fun and Fitness Council, the Colgate-Palmolive "Help Young America Campaign" with Billie Jean King and Arnold Palmer, *and* twice an ABC Women's Superstar participant. She's a special person, this Wyomia Tyus, and her mother and brothers are the first to admit they were wrong—you *can* be a lady and a sports champion.

As Willye White is. Willye is another of Ed Temple's black superstar Tigerbelles. She doesn't have an Olympic gold medal, but she has something else that makes her golden—*five* times she has been on the United States Olympic track and field team. *Five* times she has been a consistent finalist, helping keep America's records high. *Five* times she has been an Olympian, and that means being tops for sixteen years. Added to that is the fact that four years later she was an alternate for the American team. No one can top that record.

She has won an Olympic silver medal for the long jump, and another as a member of the 400-meter relay team. She has a Pan American gold in the long jump—she holds the American record in that event.

She's traveled to 150 countries as a member of thirty-five different international teams and has been inducted into the Black Sports Hall of Fame—for obvious reasons.

Willye is a licensed practical nurse and has worked in that field. She got her degree in Public Health Administration at Chicago State University and served as women's track and field coach there. At present she's Health Center Director for the Chicago Department of Health.

And if all this isn't enough to keep her busy, Willye is a consultant for the United States Olympic Job Opportunity Program and a member of the President's Commission on Olympic Sports, and belongs to a whole handful of other national and international sports committees. And she still finds time for radio and television work, and to keep speaking engagements.

She is charming, lovely to look at, capable. Her life-style, like that of others who reach the top, demonstrates what hard work can do. She has a sense of responsibility that extends from the health of international sports to the physical and mental health of her own neighbors. And she has a motto: "If you see someone without a smile, give them yours."

Willye White truly belongs with the Golden Girls.

# XII

Japan not only hosted one of the best-staged of the Olympic Games, it also produced a team that will stand forever high in the records: the Kaizuka Amazons, a fabulous, not-to-be-believed girls' volleyball team whose training surely matched that of the ancient Greek athletes.

Twenty-six hundred years ago, the best of the Greek contenders for Olympic honors were brought to Olympia. There, for ten months, they lived in dormitories called *gymnasia* (from the Greek word *gymnos*, meaning "naked"—clothes were thought to weaken an athlete). They trained under professional coaches, all day every day. For the last few weeks they lived on a diet of bread, goat cheese, and figs, then thought to be the best foods to condition them for the ordeals ahead.

Their discipline was no more severe than that of the Amazons, who lived, worked, and trained in the town of Kaizuka, about two hours from Tokyo. Like the ancient Scythian Amazons who lived in the region northeast of the Black Sea, they were unbeatable.

All the girls worked for a spinning mill in the town, much as Babe Didrikson had for a Dallas company. The mill owners sponsored the team. The girls were each paid about fifty dollars a month plus room and board. The dormitories they lived in were clean but spartan. Up at 7:00 A.M., they had breakfast and reported to work at 8:00. They stayed on the job until 3:30. Then the real work began.

In 1964 women's volleyball was included in Olympic sports for the first time. The Kaizuka coach, Hirobumi Daimatsu, was determined that his girls would win the event. And he believed in training!

A typical session began with warm-up drills, consisting of half an hour of nonstop dives, rolls, and tumbles. Next came a jarring drill that would have defeated most ordinary mortals. One by one the girls hurled themselves toward the coach, who jetted a ball out in front of the runner. She was expected to get it at any cost and that meant diving for it, landing on her chest, rolling forward, and then dashing back to repeat the process. This went on for one hour. The next hour was more of the same, but now the coach put a spin on the ball, making it tougher to get. The girls were by now gasping for breath and sodden with sweat. If one dropped to the floor exhausted, no one paid attention. They just kept on drilling and when the fallen girl got her breath back, so did she.

At 7:00 P.M. there was a hot supper, usually rice with fish. After that came scrimmage. By 10:00 the girls had had six hours of practice, and almost anyone would think that enough. Not Coach Daimatsu. To him the real test of the girls' spirit came next.

One girl stepped forward. For ten minutes Daimatsu aimed balls at her—rocket-fast balls, badly aimed balls, balls that were out of reach. Each girl had to volley them back no matter how impossible the shot seemed. When one girl finished, another took her place. And so it went.

The session ended at midnight. And the next day was the same and so was the next. Sundays were different. There was no office work then so they practiced all day. One week out of the year they were given a vacation. The other fifty-one weeks they kept to their practice sessions unless they were on tour meeting rival teams or playing a home game.

Masae Kasai, captain of the winning 1964 Olympic team, was asked by a reporter why she put up with this kind of training. She laughed. "When I want something, I try. What else should I do?"

That pretty much sums up the attitude of all

champions. Including the United States girl swimmers who captured a handful of medals at the Tokyo Games: Donna de Varona in the individual medley; Cathy Ferguson, backstroke; Ginny Duenkel, freestyle; Sharon Stouder, butterfly—all gold medal winners, with gold for the U.S. relay team as well.

There was another Golden Girl at those Games. Her name was Dawn Fraser. They called her "Granny."

Dawn was dedicated all right—dedicated to winning. But she wouldn't have endorsed the kind of training the Kaizuka Amazons relished.

"I have a different mental approach," she once said. "I enjoy training most of the time. When I don't want to work out, I don't—I don't force myself."

She was born in 1937 in Sydney, Australia, the youngest of eight children, four boys and four girls. Her father came to Australia with a Scottish soccer team, decided he liked it Down Under, got a job as a shipwright, married, and started raising a family.

He liked most sports, but swimming wasn't one of them, and there was no taking the kids for a Sunday paddle. Dawn was about five when she discovered the community pool near her home and if she'd had her way, she'd have spent most of her time there from then on.

But the family was not well off and Mrs. Fraser was ill a good deal of the time. Dawn was expected to do her share of the housework, and many of her childhood hours were spent doing chores. She swam for fun but without any serious purpose. It was her brothers who thought she was good enough to be a contestant, and they urged her to work harder.

"You could beat all the other kids," one brother told her. "You could even win some prizes."

Dawn doubted it. But when she was fourteen Harry Gallagher, one of Australia's leading coaches, saw her zipping around Drummoyne Pool. Her style wasn't much, but she had something that looked good to him, and he asked her to train under him.

That sounded exciting. Dawn talked it over with her mother, who saw immediately that this might be an opportunity her daughter could find no other way. She gave Dawn one bit of advice: "Get yourself to the top."

Dawn went to work. Three years later she had set one world record, the first of many. When the Olympics were held in Melbourne she was nineteen, "old" by today's standards. But she tore through the 100-meter freestyle in a record 1:02.0 minutes and got a gold medal.

"Too bad you didn't get started sooner," a reporter sympathized. "You could probably go to Rome in four years."

Dawn gave him a measured look. "Oh, I think I'll be there," she drawled, fingering her medal. "I'd sort of like another of these."

She was in top form when she got to Rome. She was also twenty-three, and the competitors seemed to get younger every year. She was first off the blocks in her event, and she lowered her Melbourne record by close to a second. She won the gold medal.

She also got herself banned from the team. The 400-meter relay was scheduled for the second day. Dawn had been told she wouldn't be on the team, so she went into Rome to do some shopping. She got back about noon and was just starting her lunch when she was told that the relay was scheduled to begin in forty-five minutes, and she was to swim after all.

"Well," Dawn says, "I wasn't prepared. I couldn't get prepared. And I didn't swim."

For this she was banned, but the ban was soon lifted. And Dawn started planning for the Tokyo Olympics.

It didn't look as though she would make it to those Games after all. Seven months before the opening date, she was driving home from a party with her mother and one of her sisters. The car skidded and crashed. Dawn's mother was killed, her sister badly injured. Dawn had a broken bone in her neck.

When they told her the next day, Dawn wept for her mother and prayed for her sister, who eventually recovered. The doctors told Dawn that the odds were against her ever swimming again.

But like many Olympic champions, Dawn thought that odds were to be beaten. "I had to fight back," she says. "That's what life's all about."

She fought back. And she went to Tokyo. That's

when she got the nickname Granny. Twenty-seven is certainly in the "old-lady" class for Olympic swimmers, then and now.

Dawn watched the younger swimmers practicing, and they were good—very, very good. She admitted that she tensed up.

"I'm usually pretty relaxed," she said, "but there have been other times when I've been nervous. Once in a meet in Australia I started to peel off my warm-up suit and an official stopped me. I'd forgotten my bathing suit. At another meet, I was on the starting block and I looked down and discovered I still had my socks on!" She watched another competitor skim down a practice lane. "I'll be all right tomorrow," she said.

And she was. She got her third Olympic gold medal. Granny had shown them all that she still had what it takes.


Back in the 1948 London Games another "old woman" of thirty, the mother of two, also showed that age isn't everything. Her name was Fanny Blankers-Koen, but everyone called her the "Marvelous Mama of Holland."

Fanny is the greatest woman track and field star of all times, according to most of the record keepers. Babe Didrikson was the best all-around athlete. Poland's Stanislawa Walasiewiz (known here as Stella Walsh) lasted longer. But nobody has ever beaten Mama's marvelous track and field record: world records in the 100-meter and 100-yard dashes, the 200- and 80-meter hurdles, high jump, long jump, and pentathlon. And in London four Olympic gold medals.

Fanny didn't have any coaching help until she was sixteen. Then a track coach named Jan Blankers saw her win an 800-meter race. He observed that with training she could also be a sprinter (the longer races for women hadn't been included in Olympic events at this time). He offered to coach her. Twice a week Fanny hopped onto her bicycle and made an eighteen-mile trip to his home to get his help. Within three years she was winning sprints. She had also mastered the hurdles and was winning them too. *And* she had married her coach and given birth to two children.

"People say I get my stamina and do my training washing dishes, darning socks, and taking care of the house," she laughed. "Maybe they're right."

Reporters were also saying that no thirty-year-old matron could really compete in the Olympics. Fanny disagreed with them.

"Stamina isn't just a question of a strong heart, lungs like a pair of bellows, and elastic muscles," she said. "More important is your mental attitude."

There was certainly nothing wrong with Fanny's heart, lungs, muscles, or attitude in London. By this time she held forty Netherlands championships and four world records. She wasn't about to close out her career by losing in the Olympics.

She breezed to a win in the 100-meter dash. She

took the 200-meter easily. Her third competiton was the 80-meter hurdles and, to the astonishment of everyone, Fanny was unaccountably left on the mark, all the other runners getting off ahead of her. She didn't let that faze her. She simply ran faster and took that medal, too.

But her greatest accomplishment of the day came in the relay race. Fanny was anchoring the team from Holland. The first three Dutch runners weren't as good as their competitors, and when Fanny got the baton everyone else was out there ahead of her. So, like Wilma Rudolph years later, she blazed down the track in an incomparable demonstration of her greatness. Overcoming the terrific handicap she'd been placed under, she wrested the championship for her country away from the others by barely more than a couple of inches. That was enough. Holland had won. The Marvelous Mama had won. And the press came up with a new name for her. From that day on they called her "The Flying Dutchwoman."

XIII

In the center of the vast glass-domed Olympic arena, spotlights, televison cameras, and thousands of spectators' eyes fixed on her, a tiny pixie of a pig-tailed girl stood poised, ready to begin her gymnastic floor exercise. Her name was Olga Korbut. A minute and a half later the whole world was in love with her.

This was at Munich, in 1972. There were wonderful performances during these Games. But there was also horror that shocked the world. Just before dawn on September 5, eight fanatical Arab terrorists, armed with submachine guns and grenades, scaled a security wall and blasted their way into the building where the Israeli athletes were housed. The Israeli wrestling coach, trying to block the invaders, was killed instantly. Some of the athletes escaped by breaking through the windows. But before the hours of terror were over, eleven Israelis lay dead, including nine who had been taken hostage. The terrorists, members of the secret Black September group, said their aim in this massacre had been to bring the plight of Palestinians to world attention. But the world, including a majority of the Arab people (among them those sympathetic to Palestine), was repelled by the extremists.

The morning after the murders eighty thousand people filed silently into the Olympic Stadium for memorial services. Surviving members of the Israeli team sat with the other athletes in the center of the field. The stands were draped in black and for the first time in Olympic history the flags of the 122 competing nations and the Olympic flag itself were flown at half mast. The Munich Philharmonic played the sad and solemn funeral movement from Beethoven's *Eroica*. Willy Brandt, West Germany's president, said in a shaking voice: "We stand helpless before a truly despicable act."

The Olympic Committee discussed closing the XX Olympiad, but it was decided to deny the terrorists the satisfaction of having halted the Games. What was left of the Israeli team went home to mourn its dead. The Games continued.

And so the Olympic athletes competed and many of them outdid themselves. It was, perhaps, their way of paying tribute to their massacred comrades and defying senseless acts of brutish terrorism. Many records were broken. But it was little Olga Korbut who captured the hearts and most lifted the spirits of the spectators in the stands and those watching on worldwide television.

Olga was born in the town of Grodno, USSR, near the Polish border in the Belorussian Republic. When Hitler's armies invaded the Soviet Union during World War II, Olga's town was one of the first attacked. The Belorussians fought back with tremendous courage. Over a million of them died defending their country.

Olga was, of course, not born until after that war, but her father, Valentin, then in his teens, fought side by side with the men of his village. In one battle he was gravely wounded and taken by plane over the front lines to a hospital. When he was finally released, he expected to go back to the fighting, but the Germans were in retreat. Valentin was sent to Grodno to help with the rehabilitation of the war-devastated town. It was a gigantic task. Supply systems had to be set up to bring food to the people; schools reopened; factories restored and hospitals supplied. In one of those hospitals he met a charming, pretty young woman and fell in love with her. Soon they were married.

Because so much of the town was still in ruins, Valentin and Valentina, as their friends called them, had great trouble finding a place to live. At last they located a small wooden hut and it was here that Olga and her three sisters were born. One year Valentin fell ill. He was forced to leave his position. Mrs. Korbut found work as a cook in a restaurant. It wasn't easy to bring up a family, care for her sick husband, and handle a job, too, but she managed, and the girls all helped as much as they could.

Olga was in elementary school, full of life and fun, quite able to get into mischief if there were any around, when her physical education teacher saw her potential as a gymnast. Women gymnasts (except for team competition) had not been allowed in the Olympics until 1952, and the Soviet women won a majority of the gold medals that year as well as in following Games.

Women gymnasts in these earlier years were much older than Olga and other stars of today. Maria Gorokhouska, who won in 1952, was thirty-one! At the Melbourne Olympics, four years later, the oldest gymnast was twenty-seven. Skilled and graceful as such contestants were, they didn't have the daring Olga exhibited. They did not attempt the fantastic acrobatics she did.

To accomplish them you must be fearless. And Olga Korbut was not afraid of anything.

"But she'll argue," said her coach, Renald Knysh. "And she can be stubborn as a little mule."

With her impish grin and blithe dancing steps, it's hard to think of Olga as mulish. But stubbornness is a quality that helps in gymnastics. Each move, each step of each exercise must be practiced countless times. If you slip on the bars or fall from the beam you pick yourself up and start over.

Olga was enrolled in a special sports school when her training with Knysh began. He was a big, shy man with close-cropped hair and eyes that seemed to see everything—especially the slightest mistake a pupil made. He and Olga were just about opposites in personality: she was emotional, he was quiet; she could be temperamental, he was scientific. Yet they made a great pair. Knysh was almost like a second father to Olga. He was full of innovative ideas. To him the old-style gymnastics were stiff and limiting. He introduced ballet techniques, and such hazardous moves as a backward somersault on the 10-centimeter-wide balance beam.

Olga performed this incredible move at the 1969 Soviet Championship Meet. She was only fourteen years old, and tiny for her age. The rules stated that a contestant must be sixteen to enter. But when Olga's work was reviewed, everyone agreed: she was certainly ready to compete with the best of them. The rules were amended. And Olga, the smallest and youngest of them all, was the darling of the meet. When she did her back flip, cheers and cries of astonishment filled the arena. The move also brought a rash of criticism down on Coach Knysh's head.

"A circus stunt!" the opposers cried. "Tricks of this kind don't belong in gymnastics!"

"Any move a performer can make is allowable," Knysh said firmly. "And any move can be just as difficult as the performer can manage." Knysh won the argument, and ever since that day gymnasts of world or Olympic caliber have grown more and more daring.

"Aren't you afraid?" a reporter once asked Olga.

She flipped a small hand airily. "I was a little at first. But now—never!"

Olga wasn't on the Soviet team at the World Meet the next year—her coach thought she was too young and inexperienced for such an international event, a decision that didn't please little Miss Olga a bit. After all, she'd made a hit at big Soviet meets and performed very well, too. But the decision stood. Olga went along with the team as an observer and to demonstrate some of the extraordinary new exercises Coach Knysh had devised. And even though she wasn't a contestant, she got reams of attention—pictures in the papers, stories written about her. She was everybody's favorite, and she came down with a bad case of the big head.

"I think I'd rather do it this way," she would say to her coach, as if she were quite capable of getting on without him.

He held his peace, knowing how young she was and how easily small heads can be turned. Her parents kept quiet for the same reasons. But her classmates weren't so forbearing. When she let it be known that she thought she was better than they were, they marched off and left her to her own devices.

"Who cares?" Olga sniffed, and turned up her snub nose.

And her mother said nothing. And her coach said nothing. But they waited.

Olga hurt herself in practice that spring (perhaps because she wasn't listening to instructions). She was out of training for some time. Then she fell ill and was shut away longer from her beloved gymnastics—and her teammates. She felt lonely and lost, and there was all too much time to remember how snippy she'd been, and to regret it. By the time she was well and back in training, the big head had been banished forever.

The town of Grodno had been rebuilt by this time and the Korbuts were living in a cheerful, sunny apartment. Life was much easier, though the parents' belief in work and industry was still the rule of the home. Chores must be done, schoolwork kept up. Olga was finishing elementary school now and training hard for the Munich Olympics.

Both she and her coach wanted a spectacular routine for these Games. They went to Leningrad to engage the help of a fine composer, a leading dance choreographer, and a ballet master. Together they created the routine that was to cause a sensation.

The spectators were with her from her very first appearance. Red hairbows bobbing, impish grin flashing, cool daring making them gasp, every man, woman, and child in the huge audience loved her. They held their breath when she performed her backward somersault on the beam, shouted themselves hoarse when she took flight off the uneven parallel bars, then arched downward in the "Korbut Element," her own special move, never before done by anyone else. And they booed the judges when some of the scores were not as high as they thought they should be.

No one was surprised when she won the gold medal on the balance beam. But they were stunned when, in an exercise on the uneven bars, Olga slipped—so badly that she came off the bars, losing her chance for the all-around gold.

Olga wept over that error, one she had never, ever made before in competition. It was some consolation to win a gold medal as a member of the USSR's winning all-around team.

There was one final event: the floor exercises. And little Olga Korbut, a bundle of sheer personality and tremendous skill, whirled into a routine that thrilled everyone by its brilliant virtuosity. Cartwheeling, pirouetting, whipping through chest rolls and back dives, flirting saucily with the spectators, she was matchless. The gold medal was hers.

"But I couldn't have won without my coach and teammates," she said. There was no big head at this meet.

There were souvenirs to buy for her parents, her

sisters, her little nephews and nieces. "How can Auntie Ollie go home without them?" she asked. But she couldn't set foot in a store without being surrounded by fans who wanted to touch her, get her autograph, or just wish her well. At last she resorted to a disguise: a wig and a maxi-dress. She got her souvenirs—and for herself, a stuffed toy hedgehog with purple hair.

Back home mountains of fan mail poured in from all over the world (the local post office had to hire extra help to handle it). News photographers and TV cameramen besieged her for photographs and interviews.

"What are your favorite colors?"

"Red and white—the colors of our Olympic uniforms."

"What's your favorite perfume?" (She likes many scents.) "Your favorite song?" "Your favorite boyfriend?" Olga answered all the questions put to her. It was fun being a celebrity. The United States Associated Press named her Female Athlete of the Year. Her greatest award came when she was granted the Soviet Emblem of Honor.

Enrolled now in a teacher's college, Olga was established in her own apartment and following the strict routine required of her. Her day began a little after seven when she got up and prepared her breakfast, usually including eggs or meat and fruit. And catsup. She likes it on practically anything.

After breakfast came two hours of solid training,

and then college classes until four. A late lunch (usually a thick soup). Study time. Training from six to nine and then, after a light supper (often only tea and fruit), it was off to bed at ten-thirty.

Sundays were for relaxation—"quiet times," she called them. She liked to walk in the woods, to listen to music, and to read—among her favorites, Sherlock Holmes adventures. She spent a good many hours answering her fan mail, though there was not enough time to answer it all—a fact she regretted.

And of course, following Munich there were tours with the team, and personal appearances at schools and colleges, factories and institutions. Everyone wanted to see and hear her.

In the spring of 1973, Olga, carrying her purple hedgehog, accompanied the Soviet team on a grand tour of the United States and Britain. When she stepped off the plane in New York, wildly cheering crowds greeted her. A bunch of roses so large she could scarcely see over them was thrust into her arms. Later she received the keys to the city and was guest of honor at a banquet. At Madison Square Garden twenty thousand people came to watch her and her teammates perform. In Houston she was given a ten-gallon hat that nearly swallowed her up. In Miami she and her teammates were given the run of a private beach and a free shopping trip.

"What would you like?" she was asked.

"A bikini!" She grinned. "And a pair of sandals."

That was what all the girls chose.

In Los Angeles she was mobbed by an enthusiastic group of teen-agers wearing "Olga Korbut Fan Club" T-shirts. She hadn't even known such a club existed. Now she discovered it had six hundred members! Like all the team, she loved Disneyland and was thrilled at the spectacle of Niagara Falls.

She broke her strict diet now and then on tour to munch on American hot dogs and hamburgers, ice cream and flapjacks. And, of course, catsup.

The tour was exhausting. Though training was lighter, it had to be maintained. At each of the many performances, all the girls had to give their best. But the fans always expected the most from Olga.

She was tired when the tour ended, there was no question about that. The November following the tour she entered the European Gymnastic Championships, but the strain and exhaustion had taken their toll. Olga came in second to her teammate, Ludmilla Tourischeva.

And ahead lay the Montreal Olympics. Olga would be twenty-one at those Games. And waiting in the wings was a little fourteen-year-old from Romania. A very talented new gymnast. . . .

# XIV

Who was that newcomer waiting to be seen?

Name: Nadia Comaneci (it rhymes with peach)

Age: fourteen

Weight: a mere eighty pounds

Height: four feet eleven inches

Country: Romania in southeastern Europe

And at the XXI Games in Montreal, 1976, the dramatic question soon became: Can this tiny girl win over Olga Korbut?

Nadia was born in the city of Onesti, nestled in the foothills of the Carpathians, a place of beautiful mountains and snow-fed streams. Castles stand on the mountainsides, and Count Dracula is said to have once lived in one of them.

Nadia's parents, Gheirghe and Alexandrina Comaneci, had made their home there when Onesti was a small town. Later the government turned it into a big city with new schools, factories, blocks of apartment houses, and excellent sports facilities. The Comanecis (Nadia has a younger brother, Adrian) moved into an apartment building near Nadia's school. Her father is an automobile mechanic; her mother works in a hospital.

From the time she could toddle, Nadia was a grasshopper of a little girl: jumping, running, skipping, always leaping about. She wasn't too kind to the family furniture. In three years the Comanecis had to buy four new couches because Nadia bounced on them until the springs broke! Her parents weren't exactly unhappy when she took off for kindergarten, where she could do her leaping in the school gym.

She was just six years old when she was spotted by Bela and Marta Karolyi, husband and wife gymnastic coaches at the sports school in Onesti where the best Romanian women gymnasts train. They spotted her at recess time, but before they could reach her the bell rang, and Nadia disappeared into the building with all the other children.

The Karolyis had no idea what her name was. They hustled from room to room looking for her. No Nadia. Finally Bela thrust his head through one last door and shouted, "Who in here loves gymnastics?"

Two little girls shot to their feet, shouting, "I do! I do!" Nadia was one of them. And that was the moment she began heading for the Olympics.

"At first training was like a game," she says, with her quick, fleeting smile.

"But by age eight," Coach Karolyi adds, "the student must be serious about gymnastics."

Training under the Karolyis meant working for perfection. Every day except Sunday Nadia trained for four hours. Each move on the bars, on the beam, in the floor exercises must be mastered, as a skater must master all the precise school figures. Balletlike grace must be added; more difficult moves; speed.

When she was seven, Nadia was entered in the National Championship of Romania. She placed thirteenth, excellent for such a young girl. To show how pleased they were with her, her coaches bought her an Eskimo doll. After that, at every meet she attended, she added dolls to her collection—there are now over two hundred of them lined up in her room at home. But it's the Eskimo doll that travels with her to meets.

And there were many meets to go to—and to win. In 1973 she won the Romanian championship and the Tournament of Friendship in Moscow. In London, in 1975, she won the Champions Tournament. When she was fourteen she won the European championship—the youngest girl in history to do so.

At home, Nadia, dressed in her school uniform of

navy blue jumper and light blue blouse, attended classes with twenty-five other little girls (their studies included both French and English). At two o'clock ·gymnastic training began and lasted for four hours. She worked hard; she was attentive to her coaches and very serious. No mischief, no pranks here. When she had time off she liked to zip around on her bike, swim in the summer, and ski in the winter. Sometimes she and her girl friends played soccer against the boys— and won as often as not.

From the time she started training, Nadia's goal was the Olympics. And now in July of 1976 the time had come. Her parents took her to the airport. There wasn't enough money for them to go along as they wished to. Nadia had never before gone so far from home.

"Do your best," they told her, and she nodded seriously.

"I will do well," she promised, and climbed aboard the huge plane, hugging her good-luck doll and suddenly feeling strange and lonely. Fourteen isn't so very old, after all.

In Montreal there was the hustle and bustle of getting settled in the Olympic Village, training in the unfamiliar arena with her teammates, new schedules to keep. And something else to face: here at Montreal Olga Korbut was without doubt the favorite. She was the one most of the spectators knew. She was their heroine.

In the opening day Parade of Nations Nadia marched solemnly with her teammates. Queen Elizabeth was in the royal box (her daughter, Princess Anne, was entered in the equestrian events). The torch was carried in, the flame lit. The XXI Olympiad was under way.

The first of the gymnastic competitions was called. Watching them is like watching a three-ring circus. At one end of the arena is the balance beam— 4.25 feet above the floor and about 4 inches wide; at the other end stand the uneven parallel bars. In between are the horse vault and the large orange mat used for floor exercises. All three are in use at the same time.

The crowd was calling for its favorite, chanting, *"Olga! Olga!"*

The brilliant lights of the stadium shone down on the arena. A tiny, serious-faced little girl moved to the uneven bars, stood poised a brief moment, her body motionless, her eyes deep pools of concentration. Instinctively the crowd quieted. This was the new Romanian they'd heard such rumors about. But she was hardly more than a baby! How could she possibly dethrone the champion?

And then suddenly this mere sprite of a girl was rocketing around the uneven bars, whirling and flying with incredible speed, arcing, hanging seemingly motionless in mid-air, dropping with breathless daring only to catch herself at the last split second and whirl aloft again. Her fingers seemed barely to touch the bars; her small body was a miracle of grace. "Like swimming in an ocean of air," one NBC television announcer described her performance. And he was right.

The sprite landed with perfect aplomb and flicked a smile at the spectators, who for a moment sat awed to silence, then broke into a frenzy of cheers. They quieted again. The four women judges handed their scores to the little girl messenger (no men are allowed on the floor during women's gymnastic performances—not even male coaches). The score was printed on a sign, the sign held aloft—10.0! *A perfect score!* Nadia Comaneci was perfect! Never before in the history of the modern Games had a gymnast been so judged. The spectators were on their feet cheering as though they would never stop.

The computer that must tally all scores had broken down! It hadn't been programmed to count perfect scores and it went no higher than 9.9. Experts had to be rushed in to reprogram the electronic scoreboard.

Now the word was out. "There's a great new champion gymnast! Don't miss the duel between Nadia and Olga!" Tickets were suddenly impossible to get; scalpers roamed the streets outside the stadium demanding—and getting—$100 for $16 tickets! There wasn't an empty seat in the house at any performance.

Twenty-one-year-old Olga Korbut fought back with every ounce of stamina and skill she had, but it was an anguished role for her. The exhausting tours, the inexorable years had taken too much from her. Sometimes, with the relentless eyes of television cameras on her, she looked haggard, her hair streaked with sweat, her mouth twisted grimly in a tortured parody of her famed grin.

It looked briefly as though she might recapture some of the glory that had been hers at Munich. Olga mounted the balance beam and, for a few magical moments, the pixie Olga was there again. Her body curled in a full circle; then she rose to strut in the old familiar Korbut fashion. Only the camera's eye could see the terrible strain in her face as she strove to hold a position motionless. And the crowd cheered their old favorite, and shouted her name. There were boos when the score was posted at a disappointing 9.5. But Olga, in her great bid to regain at least the medal for the balance beam, had exceeded her minute and a half and had been penalized. She would not have scored the longed-for 10.0 anyway.

Nadia was on the beam now, and the audience sat in hushed silence. She did a handstand, whirled and skipped, did perky dance steps. She did a back walkover with the coolness of a seasoned expert; cartwheels, split leaps in the air, landing without a trace of wavering. And for her dismount, she whipped through a perfect double somersault to a perfect landing. There was no question that this, too, was a perfect score. The deafening cheers went on for minutes, and

Nadia of the big brown eyes gave that fleeting smile that acknowledged the tribute.

She went on to do the impossible—if she hadn't done that already. She collected seven perfect scores (the exercises are performed more than once and scored each time before medals are awarded).

Her pianist played "Yes Sir, That's My Baby" for her floor exercise, and she was everybody's baby moving through her graceful, difficult routine. She topped off her Montreal triumph by winning her third gold medal as all-around best gymnast. (Medals are awarded for each event as well as for all-around best gymnast.)

For Olga Korbut this was the end of her brilliant reign. Such reigns must change as they always do, and every champion knows that he or she will be replaced by one who comes later. She went home to a new kind of happiness: marriage to handsome Leonid Bortkevich, vocalist with the Soviet's Union's top pop group (she'd secretly bought her wedding dress nearly a year before, in St. Louis), and she was as enchanting a bride as she had been a performer.

Nadia went home to a heroine's welcome, with thousands of Romanians storming the Bucharest airport to greet her and her teammates. At a ceremony in Bucharest's imposing new Palace of Sports and Culture, the president of Romania gave her the highest honor ever awarded by their country: Hero of Socialist Labor and the Gold Hammer and Sickle Medal.

And when all the honors and the interviews and

the television shows (including an hour-long special hosted by Flip Wilson) were over, the most famous little fourteen-year-old in the world went back to her classes—and her training. In four years the XXII Olympiad would be held in Moscow. Nadia Comaneci would be ready.

America's Cathy Rigby was an ABC sports analyst at the Montreal Games. When asked if any gymnast deserved a perfect 10.0—if the high scores given earlier performers hadn't forced the judges to award that never-before-given score—she replied: "If Nadia were doing what she did all alone in an empty room, I'd say she would still get the ten point zero."

Cathy should know. There is probably no more famous woman gymnast in America than she. Until television first captured Olga and Nadia, gymnastics were not very popular with Americans. Happily, Cathy was an exception.

Born December 12, 1952, in Long Beach, California, she weighed a minute four pounds at birth and had to put up a fight just to live.

"She and I are a lot alike," her mother once said. "She won't admit defeat in anything and neither will I."

By the time Cathy was five she was a bundle of energy and into—or onto—everything. "She was always on top of the refrigerator," her mother laughs. "If she fell off, she just scrambled back up."

Both of Cathy's parents worked, but they always

had time for the children. It was a big happy family— Cathy has two brothers and two sisters. They had a menagerie of pets: dogs, cats, a gopher, a snake, a tortoise, a monkey, and an alligator named Beauregard Frump. Every afternoon at four Cathy rushed home from school to get dinner, partly because her mother needed the help and partly because Cathy loved to cook.

All the children were sports-minded. "I never told them 'Don't do that or you'll get hurt,' " Mrs. Rigby says. There were a good many skinned elbows and shins, but there was no timidity.

Cathy taught herself to roller skate at eighteen months, and to ride a bike when she was five. She loved to turn somersaults and when she discovered the trampoline she was doing back flips after only a few tries. At eight she began ballet lessons. At ten she decided she wanted to be a gymnast. Her parents enrolled her in a recreational program where some tumbling was taught and Cathy took to it like a bird takes to flying.

But no one really took her seriously until Bud Marquette, a fine gymnastic coach, saw her grace— and her fearlessness. "You can't teach fearlessness," he says. "It has to be inborn. And you can't be a gymnast without it."

Marquette coached SCAT—the Southern California Acro Team—and to her joy he asked Cathy to join. She was just eleven years old. "In two months she learned what it took some of the others two years to learn," Marquette said. "She never fooled around."

Doll-sized, blonde, brown-eyed Cathy was headed for championship and, as in many other cases of Olympic hopefuls, that meant family sacrifices. The Rigbys were living in Los Alamitos at this time and every day her mother drove her and her sister Paula, who was also training, to Long Beach for their lessons while brother Stevie baby-sat for the youngest Rigby.

The SCATs' training ground was no sports palace. It was an old Sunday school room fitted out with equipment, some of which had seen better days. The Rigbys sold the family piano to buy uneven bars and a balance beam for their backyard so the girls could augment their practice.

Cathy trained eight hours a day, seven days a week. She watched her diet, and that was hard because she loved sweets and big spaghetti dinners. But she knew that at four-feet-eleven she must keep her weight down to about eighty-eight pounds. She wore a size 3 junior petite dress, and her coach called her "Shrimp" or "Peanut."

Cathy was winning trophies and getting experience. Every year the SCAT team toured Europe and the United States, raising donations, and Cathy was a star wherever the team went: South Africa, Japan, Scotland, the United States, England. She starred in another way in Switzerland. On their time off the girls visited a wax museum full of statues of Bluebeards and robbers and all kinds of notorious criminals. Cathy slipped under the ropes and, putting on a fierce face, posed with the statues.

She was fifteen when she went with the United States team to the Mexico City Olympics. She placed sixteenth, but she went on to win the World Cup the next year. In the 1970 World Games in Yugoslavia she won a silver medal on the balance beam, the first time an American woman had ever won in international gymnastics.

After graduating from high school she enrolled in Long Beach State College, but dropped out to concentrate on her training. In 1971 she won the gold medal at a competition in the USSR, the first non-Russian ever to do so. She starred at the World Cup Gymnastic Championships in Miami, capturing all the women's events. And during those years she was America's darling. Her picture appeared in both American and European newspapers and magazines and was on the cover of *Life*, and she was a guest on TV shows ranging from *What's My Line?* to Johnny Carson.

When it was time to choose the team for the Olympics, Cathy was our brightest hope. Then in the final trials she strained a tendon in her right foot and could not finish. The selection committee included her nevertheless, but she was out of training for several weeks.

And Munich was the "Year of Olga Korbut."

Cathy didn't get a gold medal, but she carried America to the highest place it had ever had in women's gymnastics. Her name will go down in the record books for that achievement.

Cathy retired from amateur athletics after Munich. She'd been going steady with Tommy Mason, the Louisiana-bred running back for such football teams as the Minnesota Vikings, the Los Angeles Rams, and the Washington Redskins, though with their two busy schedules it hadn't been easy to see each other half as much as they wanted to. Now, they had a simple home wedding, the kind they wanted, with loads of friends and relatives and parents all present—not to mention the family pets.

Home for the Masons is now Lake Arrowhead, high in the mountains in California, a lived-in, comfortable place, with pets and gardening and Cathy cooking up a storm whenever she's free from her professional duties.

Her top priority, Cathy says, is "to have a good family life." The family is well started with Buck, now four, who has decided at this point that he wants to be a baseball player.

Cathy's professional career is multifaceted. At the top of her interests is the gymnastic school she founded and manages in Mission Viejo, California. At gymnastic clinics, hordes of youngsters, some of them not even born when she was making headlines, crowd around her for autographs. She starred in a marvelous musical version of *Peter Pan* that toured throughout the United States, and loved every minute of it. She's appeared in such TV series as *The Six Million Dollar Man*, *The Hardy Boys*, and *Policewoman*. American TV viewers also know her through the commercials she does, where she swings through mini-routines with all the grace and skill she had in her Olympic days.

And she has been taking voice lessons for some time now. She's serious about a singing career—"ballads are my favorites," she says. Tommy, who has his own beverage distributorship near their home, uses his law background to help manage her career and is her Number One fan—except, perhaps, for all of America.

The Golden Girls of the Olympics have trained, sacrificed, displayed courage, dedicated years of their lives to reaching goals they themselves set. They've stood on Olympic winners' platforms, collected their prized medals, been warmed by spectators' cheers. But their greatest reward has always been a deeper one—the satisfaction of personal accomplishment.

There is one girl who, for personal accomplishment, stands above them all. Her name is Jill Kinmont. She never made it to the Olympics.

Everyone said she was another Andrea Lawrence, who was the only American skier ever to win two gold medals in one Winter Olympics. Jill was a cinch to make it to the 1956 Games in Cortina, Italy. Her coach, Dave McCoy, who had trained many other Olympic skiers, told her, "You're as good as on the team now."

Lithe, coppery-haired, eighteen years old, she had been working toward that goal for six years. "Skiing's my world," she declared when anyone asked her if she was ever bored with the endless training. Home for the Kinmonts was a big, foot-of-the-mountain guest ranch they owned near Bishop, California. They all worked on the ranch, and they were all ski-minded. Her father was chairman of the Far West Ski Association. Jill and her younger brother, Bobby, the National Junior Slalom Champion, competed at all the big meets: Mammoth Mountain, Aspen, Sun Valley, Jackson—wherever they were held. Her mother and small brother, Jerry, traveled enthusiastically to the meets and they had recently seen Jill win both the Junior and Women's National Slalom Championships, something nobody else had ever done.

It was January 30, 1955, the day for the pre-Olympic ski tryouts at Alta, Utah. Flurries of powdery snow whipped into the air from Rustler Peak; the sun was brilliant. Jill felt terrific, keyed high but not nervous, the feeling athletes get when they know they're in top form and raring to meet the competition. Her picture had just been on the cover of *Sports Illustrated*, and Dick Buek, a champion daredevil skier who very obviously liked her, had called her a glamourpuss. She wished that skier Bud Werner had been the one to give her that compliment. She was in love with him and though they weren't exactly engaged, they had an understanding. He'd be watching her today, and that made her very happy. Fleetingly, she thought of her brother, who was skiing in a match at Kratka Ridge— Jerry and her parents were with him.

"Good luck," she said silently, as they'd said to her before they took off.

Now the giant slalom was called and Jill put everything else out of her mind. Andrea Lawrence was in this race and Jill knew she was the one to beat.

Mentally she ran through the course. She was sure she knew it. The starting signal came. She surged forward, crouching low, barreled through the swooping turns on the upper part of the course. She found herself slipping low on a gate (the pairs of poles slalom skiers must snake through), recovered, and shot toward the trees where the corkscrew turn was. She was moving terribly fast, about forty miles an hour. A four-foot-high knoll lay ahead. She got ready to pre-jump it so she would land on its top and then ski down. Her timing was off. She jumped late, and suddenly she catapulted off the top of the knoll. She was flying, twisting desperately in the air trying to avoid the trees and the spectators. She crashed, slid, spun, tumbled another fifty feet, slammed into a spectator and carried him with her as she cartwheeled down the mountain. She landed on her neck, plowed to a stop. And lay there.

She was conscious. She saw the horrified faces of the people who had rushed to her. She heard someone say, "*Don't move her!* Get a litter! Get splints!"

Jill could not feel the snow beneath her, and she should have. She found she could move her head, and that was all she could move. The rescue team raced up. Someone put a hand on her.

"I can't feel you!" she whispered. "I can't feel anything!"

They got her to a hospital in Salt Lake City as fast as the ambulance could make it. For days she hovered between life and death. Holes were bored in each side of her skull and vicelike tongs plugged into them to hold her head rigid. She lay strapped to a strange bed, a canvas-covered metal frame on an axle that allowed her to be turned regularly. Doctors and nurses were in constant attendance.

Slowly . . . slowly . . . the critical stage passed. She would live. And then Jill Kinmont had to learn the truth—the stark, inescapable, terrible truth: she would never ski again. Never walk. She was paralyzed from the shoulders down—a quadruple paraplegic. Perhaps she would regain partial use of her hands, possibly a little movement in one arm. There was no guarantee.

It was a stunning blow for this girl—this vital, life-loving girl—to absorb. The truth sank in slowly as realization grew. She would never dance again . . .

never ride horseback, roaming the ranch she loved so much ... never dress herself ... or tend her bodily needs ... never ... never....

The enormity of it was numbing. As its full meaning grew clearer, she had times of fear and despair. What would she do? How would she live? How did anyone manage? She forced the fears aside. She would not think of all she had lost. She would think of what she had left. She remembered a bear cub she had once seen using his paws so cleverly ... if she could use her hands like that, if she could get them to work even a little, she wouldn't be totally helpless.

So Jill Kinmont set her new goal and struggled toward it. Little by little. Bit by incredibly hard-won bit ... tongs removed ... steel brace to replace it ... Right hand useless. Left-hand fingers permanently cramped clawlike together. But a muscle in that wrist had life! *Work on it!* That muscle in the left arm ... *make it obey your will to lift!* Make it respond—even just quiver.... Learn to sit in the wheelchair they put you in. Don't bend your head forward. You have no back muscles to hold you upright, you'll collapse face down! *Work ... Work ...*

Well-wishers from all over the country sent messages. Friends visited. Dick Buek came often—and often at unexpected times, as though he sensed when she was low. He teased her and kidded her—never, never looked at her with the pity that was so hard to bear. He was like a tonic.

"Hey, what a challenge! Hey, you're terrific! Hey, doll, you're beautiful!"

Bud Werner came, too. He tried to pretend the accident made no difference. But she saw his eyes shift away from her, heard the strain in his voice, and knew, painfully, that he could never again feel the same about her. The word *cripple* stood like a glass wall between them. And always would—she knew that. So, hiding the hurt that stabbed inside her, she released him quietly from their understanding. She said good-bye . . . she sent him away . . . she wept by herself when no one could see . . . .

And she worked . . . worked . . . worked . . . And made jokes at her clumsiness . . . Laughed at the mishaps. . . .

Costs mounted. They were enormous. The guest ranch they had all worked so hard to establish had to be sold. There were no regrets shown by parents and brothers—they were a family, together as they always had been in whatever came to any of them. Her father and older brother took paying jobs. Her mother worked one of the eight-hour hospital shifts daily to save a nurse's salary. The Far West Ski Association, the Shriners, home-town friends made donations. Still the debts mounted.

But Jill *was* making progress—small, barely discernible bits of progress. And each was a triumph. She could bend her wrist just a little more today . . . she'd moved her arm up two inches. . . .

"Look at you, baby!" Dick cried. "Hey, you're a winner!"

She quipped with reporters who came to write sad stories about her, was frank about the extent of her injuries, answered their questions. They had just one complaint: "She's so damn cheerful—we can't get a picture of her when she's not smiling!"

Oh, she had endless times of frustration—and some of sheer rage. Not to be able to comb her own hair, or put on lipstick, or scratch her nose when it itched! Never to be able to bend down and pick something up from the floor. Such things were infuriating . . . and frightening, too. . . .

But Jill didn't brood over them. She set her mind on what she *could* do, and said, "I will!"

And she did. With a device strapped to her wrist she learned to write—huge letters at first, and then smaller, neater. Through hours of therapy and practice far more exacting and difficult than any ski training had been, she learned to move her left arm upward (gravity pulled it down for her). She learned to eat with something called a spork (half spoon and half fork) that fit over her thumb and forefingers, and cussed or howled with laughter when mashed potatoes or chocolate pudding landed in her ear instead of her mouth. Moved after thirteen months from the hospital to a rehabilitation center, she struggled for over a year to master the few crucial skills left her.

"Boy!" she exults. "The day I could wash my own face—now that *was* a triumph!"

It was only one of the unbelievably difficult triumphs she was to win. She was fiercely determined to become financially independent—she was constantly aware of what her care was costing her family, though no one ever thought of complaining, and she'd made up her mind that she was going to be a contributor, not just a user. In spite of the fact that she had to be lifted in and out of a car, wheeled to her classes, helped with her books—in spite of the fact that it took her twice as long as anyone else to do her school papers and she had to be granted extra time to complete an exam, she entered the University of California and earned her B.A. Not only that, she won a scholarship for summer studies in Vienna, reported on the Winter Olympics at Squaw Valley for a Los Angeles paper, and worked as a volunteer for John F. Kennedy's presidential campaign.

*And* she went skiing! Strapped to her wheel chair, the chair bolted to skis, friends gave her a push and she went whooshing down gentle slopes, whooping with glee. Weekends Dick settled her in his sportscar and raced to Mammoth Mountain for reunions with friends, for cookouts and parties. He took her up in his plane; wrote zany letters when he was absent; gave her speed races in her wheelchair (the doctors decried them; Dick and Jill loved them). He asked her to marry him, and would take only yes for an answer. They were terribly happy.

And then Dick . . . exuberant, gentle, life-celebrating Dick Buek was killed in a plane crash.

And another "never" was added to Jill's life . . . Never to see him again . . . never to hear his voice shouting happily, "Hey, you're terrific!" Never to marry him . . .

Jill absorbed the blow with the same courage she had shown since her accident. She was quieter now, a little more withdrawn. Much of her effort was concentrated on earning her teaching degree, for Jill had decided her future lay this way. She wanted to teach children who had problems—she knew a lot about *them*.

She applied for graduate work in teacher's training at the University of California in Los Angeles. Her application was rejected! Jill appealed the decision over and over again until she had gone to the highest authorities. The rejection remained. "Elementary school teachers must be able to walk up and down stairs," they ruled. "Obviously, you can't."

"And they had me there," Jill said flatly.

But they hadn't stopped her. Stopping Jill Kinmont was not that easy. The family moved to Washington and she applied to a university in Seattle. She was accepted. She got her degree. And she got the teaching job she wanted!

"We feel lucky to have her," the superintendent said. "She's an asset to our school system."

One job wasn't enough. Summers Jill returned to Bishop, California, and there she organized, launched, and taught special reading classes for the disadvantaged Paiute Indian children, who responded like eager puppies. At first school was a small workroom in the back of a church. The second year the Tribal Council raised enough money to build a study center, where Jill presided happily.

"I'm not just a teacher," she says, "I'm part of the tribal family." A very loving family . . .

And so Jill Kinmont, Olympic hopeful, paraplegic, indomitable spirit, and beautiful woman, reached her goal. It wasn't the one she had aimed for at first; it was far more difficult to reach than any she had ever dreamed of, but she reached it gallantly and found in it deep satisfaction, warm and personal.

Today Jill Kinmont is married to a gentle, caring man named John Boothe and they make their home outside Bishop, the small, friendly town where Jill grew up. On their five acres of land they raise calves, John has a thriving vegetable garden, and Jill has her flowers. "I love them," she says. "I couldn't do without them."

Jill, now in her fifteenth year of teaching, works with elementary-school children with reading disabilities. Summers she teaches her Indian children. John owns and manages an equipment rental company and a service station. They have a trailer, specially equipped for Jill's needs, and take many vacation trips in it. Jill fills as many speaking engagements as time permits.

"I go anywhere they ask me," she laughs, "from

the Spinal Cord Injury Unit in a hospital to an eighth-grade graduation in a one-room schoolhouse." The life of Jill and John Boothe is full and happy, yeasty with plans. There is always something more to accomplish.

Two movies and a TV special have been made about Jill. Books, magazine articles, and news feature stories have told of her life. She was a ski champion that day on the mountain. Since that day—that nearly fatal day that stripped her of so much—she has become far more: a symbol of courage and an inspiration.

Babe Didrikson . . . Wilma Rudolph . . . Galina Zybina . . . Jill Kinmont . . . all of those written about here are Golden Girls. Not for their medals. Not for the headlines they made or the cheers echoing around them. Not even for their talents. But because in each there was that special something that made them want to achieve and the will to accomplish.

That's what makes them Golden . . . what makes them important . . . what makes them worth knowing. And well remembered.

# INDEX